Maryland's Eastern Shore
A Place Apart

Volume II

Queen Anne's, Talbot, Caroline and Kent Counties

by

Jacqueline Heppes Baden

Maryland's Eastern Shore, A Place Apart
Volume II
Queen Anne's, Talbot, Caroline and Kent Counties

Jacqueline Heppes Baden
Cover Design & Illustrations by the Author
Published 1990
Travel On Tape
Book Division
517 Nelson Street
Rockville, Maryland 20850
First Edition
Copyright 1989
Jacqueline Heppes Baden
All Rights Reserved

Printed in the United States
BookMaster Inc.
638 Jefferson Street
P.O. Box 159
Ashland, Ohio 44805

Library of Congress Catalog
Card Number 89-051970
ISBN 0-9624619-3-8

PREFACE

What would Maryland's Eastern Shore be like if the Chesapeake Bay Bridge had not been built? It was suggested, in a letter to the editor run in The Baltimore Sun in 1949, that instead of building the Chesapeake Bay Bridge, officially named the William Preston Lane Memorial Bridge, the state should just give the Eastern Shore to Delaware and save fifty million dollars.

In 1842, 1850 and again in 1883 there were thoughts on the Shore of seceding from the Union and forming the new state of Delmarva, joining with Delaware and Virginia. Fortunately this radical idea was voted down but only by a margin of five to four.

One can speculate that the Shore, as the new state of Delmarva, might have remained the same and all that is there to see and to do might not be there. That Ocean City might still be the small seaside resort it was in the early 1900s, but there is no need to speculate because, when the Bridge opened in 1952, the Shore changed for better or for worse, but forever.

Today nine hundred thousand sports fishermen fish the Bay's waters, along with a quarter of a million sports crabbers, thirteen thousand licensed watermen, who crab, and five thousand watermen who hunt the elusive oyster.

Volume II of Maryland's Eastern Shore, A Place Apart, is the second in a planned series on places apart in Maryland. Volume I, Worcester, Wicomico, Somerset and Dorchester Counties, was published in June 1990.

QUEEN ANNE'S COUNTY

HER ROYAL HIGHNESS' COUNTY

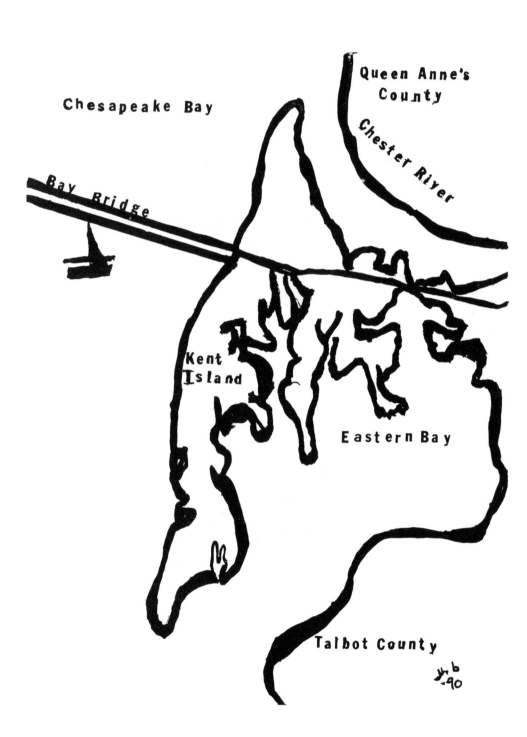

QUEEN ANNE'S COUNTY

Across the Chesapeake Bay Bridge is Queen Anne's County, the gateway to the Eastern Shore. Queen Anne has never been there, however, her Royal Highness, Princess Anne was there to celebrate the two hundred and seventy-first anniversary of the founding of the County in 1706. Queen Anne's County is the crown jewel of the Chesapeake, just ask the princess.

Kent Island, the first solid ground after crossing the Bay, takes the form of a giant crab's claw and enclosing Eastern Bay makes a bay within a bay. The island is low and flat, barely above water. In the early morning you hear the soft coo-coo of the doves, the screeching squeal of the herring gulls, and after dark, you are enclosed by a black velvet sky sparkling with stars falling below the horizon. As you drive along the Isle of Kent, you might remember Captain William Claiborne.

The captain was a man, who when he saw something he wanted, went after it with all the tenacity of a male lion protecting his pride. He was a man with definite ideas who fought determinedly all his life for the return of "his" island. You see this Isle of Kent was once all his, every bit and more.

Claiborne landed on Kent Island in 1629 and by 1631 the island was the site of the first English settlement in Maryland. (St. Mary's City was established in 1634.) Claiborne was an aristocrat from Great Britain who did not believe in roughing it. When he came he brought with him a number of vessels loaded to the gunwales with his possessions and a female servant. Joanne Young was the first white woman in the New World and was brought along to "do his linen," as Claiborne put it.

The captain came from Virginia to look around, much like Captain John Smith. The view of Kent Island from the mouth of the Chester River so much reminded him of Westmoreland, his home in England, and of an estuary of the Kent River there, that he named the island Kent.

Claiborne's name comes up in one way or another in the history of all the counties which touch the Bay. His influence was widely felt, and his angry voice heard. Claiborne, at one time, possessed what was first referred to as the "Isle and County of Kent." This title encompasses all that was between the Bay and the Atlantic Ocean as far north as the state of Delaware.

In 1642 Kent Island was formed into a county, called Kent Island County, and the upper part of what is now Queen Anne's and Kent Counties were a part of this decision. Previous to this, Cecil, Lord Baltimore, had taken part of Claiborne's land to form Talbot County, then Kent and Talbot were the whole Shore. In 1706 a goodly part of Kent was lost and Queen Anne's County was born. (Long live the Queen!)

The land near the water was settled first and understandably so. The Choptank Indians began to complain about this invasion of palefaces, for what good it did them. There was a fort built on the island and folks lived inside the stockade in drafty log cabins whose chinks were filled with mud and mortar and looked tacky. No hand-pegged, random-width, hardwood floors, all were clay (a nice word for dirt). You huddled around the fireplace and stirred the stew in the iron pot, or when you slept, you crawled into your bearskin spread on the floor. Life was tough and rough and so were the settlers.

It wasn't long though before there was a kiln and bricks were fired and glazed a russet color, and manors were built. These manors in no way resemble the manors of later years, but were sturdy and luxurious for those days. Many are still standing in Queen Anne's County.

Claiborne knew value when he had it. Kent Island had location. (He should have sold real estate.) He also knew how to run a business. Under his iron domination, the trading post he started and the settlement were represented in Virginia's House of Burgesses. His power was imperiled when King Charles I granted the Maryland Charter to Sir George Calvert, the first Lord Baltimore. Claiborne flatly refused to give up his land and this attitude brought him great grief. In an attempt to appease Claiborne, he was given the right to hold the land as a **tenant,** but not as lord.

Clever Claiborne had a case all right. After all, he received a license in 1631 from the King to trade and make decisions, hadn't he? Yes he had. Duplicity played a role in Claiborne's loss of his island kingdom. One of his own, Captain George Eveline, surrendered Claiborne's "army" while Claiborne was in England on business. Within a year, the Lord Commissioners in London ruled that Baltimore had title to Kent Island.

Not of faint heart, Claiborne snuck back to the island in 1644 and brought about a coup d'etat, while Governor Calvert, Lord Baltimore's brother, was away. Claiborne got only a two-year reprieve before he was obligated to make a getaway to Virginia. All in all, Claiborne had a deep and all-encompassing love for Chesapeake Country and Kent Island which consumed him for the rest of his life. When he was nearly ninety, he once again made a pitiful request of the Crown for the return of "his" island. The scoundrel, Captain Eveline, got his "reward" and became Commander of Military Affairs.

In 1637 the island was divided, in the old English way of hundreds, and this was to stand until other counties on the Shore were formed. The remains of Claiborne's trading post, fort and dwellings are presumed to be under the waters of Eastern Bay. (Time and tide.)

Before you return to Route 50, stop and see the grassy churchyard which is "alive" with the dead. That is to say, haunted. You would haunt folks and float restlessly around at night, too, if you had been cozy in your grave and some young'ns came along and moved your church. The site of Christ Church is where the oldest church in Maryland used to be. No more, the church was moved to Stevensville in 1880.

The dead however are right there where they were interred, at the end of a gravel road in a grove of tall trees enclosed by a wood fence. Do not walk on the graves! The graveyard is purported to be possessed by ethereal beings and walking on the graves would certainly disturb these spirits, who might then disturb you. The whole island seems haunted by Claiborne whose prints are indelibly marked in the sands of time.

The captain would be stunned by how "his" island has caught on. Kent Island is showing some changes, as all places with a water view do. Enclaves of condos have choice spots on the water, and along Route 50 it is sheer bedlam. There are three towns of note on the island, Dominion, very small; Chester, growing fast; and Stevensville, grown and returning to the past as fast as can be.

You know where Stevensville is, you've just never stopped. You can't miss the odd, two-story, square structure with the oversized widow's walk on top, which once was the schoolhouse antique emporium and before that a school. This old landmark is freshened with paint as is all of Stevensville, a town with a new, old face. Stevensville is not updating, but returning to the past.

Stevensville is a bit of "Queen Victoria" in Queen Anne's County. This hamlet is gradually moving back in time to become a Victorian village, again. A feeling of unreality is part of being in Stevensville.

There is no problem parking. Park anywhere and then step back to what was and is hoped will be again, the town of yesterday. The old homes are shabby, but respectable, antique ladies who are getting a face lift. The done-over downtown is pictured on the cover of the

11

October 1987 issue of the National Trust for Historic Preservation's publication. The scene depicts folks intently watching a parade going by, sitting in yard chairs on the new red brick sidewalk in front of the old bank building, which is decorated with patriotic bunting.

The "downtown," a half dozen old buildings and a number of brand new condos built to look old, are all painted yummy colors of orange, lemon, and mint, making them especially appealing. The bank opened for business in 1907, a brass plaque on the side of the stucco building lets you know this. Cup your hands and peek through the glass windows of the double front doors. You will see a half circle of golden oak which forms the counter where three tellers could cash your check. There is room for nothing else. The gleaming steel door of the safe gapes open and you realize there is no money in the bank, no more.

You could cross the street, no traffic light needed (nor is one supplied), to the other side and buy a stamp in the post office if it were still a post office, which it is not. This miniature doll house size structure is edged all along the roof line with scalloped trim making the old post office look like one of those gingerbread houses you make at Christmastime.

The Cray House is the home of the Kent Island Historical Society, the pride of the historic district and rightfully so. It is around the corner on Cockney Lane (cute name). The one hundred and eighty-five year old house is a snug dwelling, that sits on a tract of land known as "Steven's Adventure." (More about what adventures Steven had, if the author can find out; if not, no more. After all, the land was granted to Francis Steven in 1694, and no one is around who knew him.)

The house tilts a bit and who wouldn't after standing so long. The deep green roof is sloped steeply down over half of the first level, making it another of those so-called "eyebrow" houses. (Eyebrow houses are characterized by windows on the second floor which are only one half as large as normal windows.) The structure is soundly built of three-inch thick, solid

planks about fifteen inches wide and mortared and pegged into posts. She may be sagging in her old age, but she will never tumble down; she is built to last through the centuries. The ancient dwelling is enclosed by a white picket fence, perfect for its Dutch roof. In the backyard is a dilapidated darling, the old Love Point Train Station, which served as a railroad and ferry terminal connecting Baltimore with the Pennsylvania Railroad Line to Rehoboth, Delaware. Plans are to renovate it sometime...

Christ Church, which used to be next to the haunted graveyard, is impressive. A Gothic looking affair with a freestanding bell tower on one side and on the other a lancet (an acutely put arch) chimney. (Just the word Gothic conjures up images of ghosts and spooks, doesn't it?)

Outside of Stevensville, along Love Point Road as you head toward the Point, there is a concrete company that has a remarkable sign in front. It is about 4' x 6', painted white and lettered in red. The words are an epitaph. "A tribute to Bobby Snyder, Sr. A hard working man and a good friend. We will miss you... Gone, but not forgotten." The land below the sign is outlined with 2" x 4"'s, a small tree grows behind it and you think the enclosure must be Bobby's grave, but no...he is in the cemetery with everyone else. (What more can you say about something as touching as this except Bobby was certainly loved?)

Smokey Joe, a favorite among the steamboats, puffed back and forth from Love Point to Baltimore carrying locals to spend a day in the big city and "foreigners" to the railroad terminal that whisked them to the beach in Delaware. You paid your 50 cents, bought a round-trip steamboat ticket and went above to the top deck. Cars and trucks were loaded in four lanes on the lower deck. She made twenty trips a week, three times a day.

Now, you didn't simply lean on the steamboat's rail and watch the wake. There were slots, one-armed bandits, for a penny, and crap for a sawbuck. The dice game was for the "big boys." The real bargain, besides the fare, was fresh produce loaded on trucks headed for

Baltimore's Lexington Market. You could haggle with the farmers for fresh produce and everyone's favorite, the succulent Eastern Shore melons.

Lots of folks liked to dine at "Miss Mary's," a tiny hotel which used to be on Pier Road above the ferry slip. Fried chicken, natch, and soft-shell crab in season were the favorites. (For those who have never tried this crustacean fried in total and served with its legs sticking out from the sides of a bun and its vacant eyes staring up at you, don't look! Just slather it with tarter sauce or cocktail sauce, more favored on this side of the Bay Bridge, and bite in, delicious and crispy good.) To go on with the meal, corn on the cob fresh from the fields, stewed tomatoes, Maryland beaten biscuits (little golf ball sized crumbly dough balls that taste like sawdust and must be washed down with a brew or two...the author's opinion, not offered in some circles on the Shore) and extra rich and creamy ice cream for dessert. This feast cost you a dollar. On Saturday nights the dance at the Love Point Hotel drew a real big crowd; if you were so inclined you could stay over. It was a sad night when the hotel burned. Stevensville will never again know the high old time of the Gay Nineties and the Roaring Twenties, none of us will, but Stevensville **will** always have her precious memories.

To regroup and regain your composure after passing through the endless array of commercial enterprises and the big discount centers along Route 50, and before Queenstown, drive out Bennett Point Road along the Wye River.

A collage of spectacular architecture makes these big-buck estates (you would never call them simply homes) worth a look. They are all huge, and all have water views, many with piers and boats (sorry, yachts). It is a stunning display of wealth, this complex of homes with architecture from the eighteenth century to some which qualify as space age or the twenty-second century.

The Wye is really two rivers dividing just above the mouth at Bennett Point. (This is why the river is named Wye because it forms a Y!) From the road you can see the island, now a natural resource management area where farmland, forest and wildlife coexist under the management of the University of Maryland. The idea of coexistence came from Judge John Beale Bordley, a man with a passion for self-sufficiency, for an independent environment.

Bordley retired to Wye Island after serving as an Admiralty Judge in Annapolis, and began to put his idea of independence together. On his farm he had a kiln powered by a huge windmill of his own design which furnished power. He imported cattle and sheep to have meat to eat and wool to wear. He grew flax and cotton used for clothing. Hemp provided rope. The garden grew everything possible in the climate and that was a lot. Herbs to spice, salt to season, bees to sweeten, a tannery for leather and grapes for wine, were all there. His favorite was his special brew, a beer that was his pride and joy. Bordley supplied flour, fruits and vegetables to the Continental Army without waiting for a requisition. His life, though he was a patriot, was dedicated to the improvement of the methods of husbandry. He wrote a book in which he included all his ideas and some favorite recipes, one of which was for ice cream.

"Two pewter basins, one large, the other small, the small one to have a close cover; in this basin the cream is put and mixed with strawberries, to give flavor and color; sweeten it. Cover it close, and set the small basin in the large one. Fill this with ice and a handful of salt, to stand for three-quarters of an hour; then uncover and stir the cream well together; over it close half an hour longer, and then it may be turned out onto a plate." (The way the word "close" is used in the above quote is the way one spoke in the 1700s, apparently. Please don't blame the author!)

A group of citizens met in Queenstown and burned a copy of the Stamp Act, shot off cannons and drank twenty-three toasts to freedom. (Driving under the influence wasn't a problem then.) Queen Anne's County provided "necessities" when a ship was sent from the Eastern Shore to Boston to relieve "the suffering brethren of Boston." Two companies of militia were formed from Kent and Queen Anne's. The troops were ordered to the Northampton Courthouse on Virginia's Eastern Shore, where the enemy was well fortified. They didn't stay long.

However, the mobilization of the troops caused the British to delay their attack, a move which helped win the war. The Queen Anne's Militia, along with others from the Shore, fought in the Battle of Long Island sustaining heavy losses. Even after Cornwallis surrendered at Yorktown, Queen Anne's still had a problem with the Tories. Plans to burn Bordley's estate on Wye Island were foiled. A number of articles of great value were stolen, but later returned. To protect themselves from such pillaging, a group of men equipped a large barge with armament, and with twenty aboard went to fight the traitors. Things settled down after this and peace was restored.

The War of 1812 affected Queen Anne's County only after the seizure of the packet Jefferson by the British on April 16, 1813. The troops were called up for fear that the Redcoats would soon be upon them.

Major William Nicholson had two hundred and forty-four men under his command who were ready to defend Queenstown in the event of a British attack. Captain Gustavus Wright had readied a company of artillery men, and Major Emory commanded a cavalry of one hundred and had two six-pound cannons. A battery was thrown up to protect Queenstown as soon as they heard that the British had landed on Kent Island with no resistance from the patriots.

Nicholson, who feared the enemy might attack from the rear, withdrew to Slippery Hill, ordering his men not to fire. To his great dismay a soldier or two got off a few shots. Two English were killed, five wounded and General Snyder Beckwith's horse was shot out from under him. The Redcoats took the town with ease. Queenstown seemed to have little importance after the capture and outside of taking some beef and bacon and a few supplies, they left the city untouched.

While all of this was going on, the residents of Centreville were erecting a forty-foot battlement just below town along the banks of the Corsica River. The

Redcoats, approaching by water, saw what they mistakenly thought might be a fort and made for the opposite side of the river, and set up temporary headquarters. There was never any contact with British troops whose officers considered the action on the Eastern Shore only a diversion for nuisance value. This spot is known as "Fort Point" and is enshrined in the minds of those later generations as the almost sacrosanct ground where Centreville was delivered from the hands of the enemy.

Queenstown blossomed after the war and at one time had it all. Queenstown Creek was navigable and cargos of grain, hemp and tobacco left for Europe and manufactured goods arrived. The wealthy planters along the river stimulated the growth of the county seat and the port was, at this time, considered to be the chief port on the Eastern Shore.

Oh, it was nice. People came regularly since the town was on the way to the Bay Bridge and hence across to the "other side." There were road signs, even then. A notch hacked out of a tree along the roadside meant this way to the ferry across the Bay, two notches with another above, on trees on both sides of the road, meant the courthouse was there just around the bend, God willing. Queenstown began to dwindle when the county seat was moved to Centreville. On November 11, 1820, Queenstown burned in a blaze which destroyed all the wooden buildings, which meant almost the entire town.

The mood before the Civil War broke out was one of tolerance in terms of the preservation of the Union and moderate measure was taken in regard to slaves. Queen Anne's was slaveholding and many meetings were held with the intention of preventing any interference with the status quo. The Methodists, who had converted lots of souls in Queen Anne's, were strong in their beliefs about the institution of slavery and its evils, took an unpopular stand. However, it was the Methodists and their desires for a peaceful settlement, who were influential in keeping the County in the Union. There was talk of secession. The thought of gathering a militia to put down any slave uprisings was considered but never implemented.

Wye   Island

When the War began plans were made to set up recruiting stations in order to fill the quota assigned by the federal government. Not much else happened during the Civil War in this peaceful place far from the battlefields. Some few prominent persons were imprisoned for their attitudes. There was a great deal of empathy for Richard Bennett Carmichael, a judge in Talbot County, who was arrested for treason while actually sitting on the bench, and badly beaten, but nothing came of it. He was released.

After the Civil War, folks in Queenstown returned to the social life and parties became even more lavish and duels more common. Slippery Hill, the place where the army retreated in the War of 1812, became a place where men met on the field of honor.

Gustavus Wright and the man who called him "out" faced each other only six feet apart and took careful aim. The man was shot in the hand and in the side; Wright wasn't hit at all. Gustavus was a spitfire kind of guy. He had his reputation to uphold, after all, he often boasted, when he was only twelve years old he was a second for his father, Robert Wright, when he dueled with Governor Lloyd.

Custom had it when one party took the risk of letting the other fire first, he was then allowed to approach as near as he wanted to get off his shot. Governor Lloyd was a marksman and took the advantage. He stood almost nose to nose with Robert Wright and said, "What are you going to do, sir? Your life is in my hands!" The then noisy kid, Gustavus, shouted, "Tell him to shoot, Pa, and be damned!" However, no blood was shed.

When Gustavus grew up he killed a man in a duel. His brother, Clinton, wasn't so skilled and he was shot by a Major Hook, but not killed. The major had suggested that they lie side by side on the ground and fire again. The seconds resisted this notion, stating that duelists must remain standing. Clinton, following in the family tradition of foolhardy bravery, demanded that he be tied to a tree. Wonder of wonders, both duelers survived!

On Wye Island, shortly before it became an environmental area, there were twelve farms. You got there over a bridge at one end or by ferry at the other. The farms were profitable, it was good tillable soil and wheat sprouted in the fields. Lots of ripe wheat needs cutting and that requires a threshing rig and hands to pitch the hay. There is a story about how the workers wanted a particular Saturday afternoon off to go to town, but because the job wouldn't be done until sundown, the owner told them they couldn't go. When the boss looked away, a heavy wrench landed in the works of the thrasher and everyone went to town. After that, the workers got every Saturday afternoon off.

Farm life on the island was lots of work and little play, as was true of life on farms all over the United States and still is. The women raised chickens while the men did the field work. The refrigerator was a window box in winter; and in the summer, a basket down the well. Lanterns filled with kerosene gave light. Every year you yanked the old musty straw from your mattress and refilled it with fresh sweet hay. Your pillow was a goose-feather tick which needed to be puffed up every morning. Nothing could keep 'em down on the farm and the farms disappeared.

Wye Island is one of those haven heavens unsullied by the rupture of the bulldozer. It is spoken of in hushed tones by those who know what is there and who hope to keep what is there to themselves.

What is there? Two thousand eight hundred and fifty acres of virgin forest, hedgerows cutting zigzag across fields and dusty paths meandering through a remote wilderness of song birds, wild animals and past twenty-one miles of beach, is what is there.

Although only a short distance from Route 50, Wye Island is as sequestered as any virgin in a nunnery. To spend a day where a white-tail deer only looks at you curiously, but knows no fear, where the red fox eyes you from the tall grasses, where warblers warble and goldfinch flutter their black wings and woodpeckers peck at the hardwood trees, is to be in the enchanted forest. You too may visit. The old bridge is still the way, but not for long, a new spectacular span is planned.

There are picnic tables on the high banks of Grapevine Cove where the winds whisper to you of men such as John Bordley who walked these trails over two hundred years ago.

The normally placid Wye River can kick up .her heels if she's a mind and swallow up a boat with one good wave. On an icy winter day some time back, a blustering nor'easter hit with raging winds and stupendous seas. Some along the shoreline tell about how they saw a tall-masted ship with tattered sails rolling dangerously close to capsizing with every wave that hit her. The screams for help from the mariners could hardly be heard over the shriek of the howling winds. When dawn's light cut the darkness with a scarlet streak and the sky was clear and blue and the wind had gone to bed, the ship had vanished, and was never seen again. When the weather is especially calm, there is a luminous phosphorescence on the water which traces her path up the river. Local lore has it that this glowing substance is a ghostly remembrance of the ship and her crew.

Ghost ships are legend the world over, and so it is on the Eastern Shore. Here is another. The Willie Bennett was a ship with a huge mast of loblolly pine that towered forty feet above the deck. She was something, this ship with her white hull gleaming in the sunlight and her sails blossoming full in the breeze.

A rough and tumble crew worked her decks. It seemed that one day an argument came up between the captain and the hands over the price for oysters, which he had recently sold. A fracas broke out, and in the melee, the skipper was killed. Sometime after this disaster, the Willie Bennett was discovered sailing around all by herself. There wasn't a single mariner aboard. The Willie Bennett remained in service until 1963 with a crew and captain who **were** aboard, in spite of her ability to sail herself.

You will see a sign, on down Route 50 where you come off Bennett Point Road, which says Queenstown, so close to the highway yet so few turn off. As late as the 1920s, there were three wharves, the ferry boat

COLONIAL COURT HOUSE QUEENS TOWNE

Jhb
'90

dock, the landing where you drove your car aboard and a wharf used by the railroad. There was a drug store, a barber shop, a grist mill and a gas station. The Queen Theater played Gene Autry movies every Saturday night. Homewood Inn was busy with guests and the Queenstown News was read by everyone. The "Toonerville Trolley," an old bus, took folks from Centreville to catch Smokey Joe at Love Point. Everyone ate country ham and turncakes at Mr. Will Lane's Wheatlands.

When you hear about Queenstown, you will be scandalized by the goings-on when she was the seat of government. They swung 'em high from the gallows, branded them with a set of codes to be revealed later and whipped bare backs, all in the name of puritan justice.

On August 18, 1706, the General Assembly created the "Queen" and stipulated that "...the County shall enjoy all rights and privileges equal with the other counties of the province." Thirteen commissioners got together and purchased two acres to be used as the site of the courthouse "for continuing the County Court of Queen Anne's at Queens-Towne."

One soul kept a journal in which he tells us that a courthouse was built in 1708, the date appearing on each end of the building. Next to come was a jail, and Colonel Richard Tilghman got the contract to build the pokey "for the use of the County." He received ten thousand pounds of tobacco for his time and trouble in building the gaol. (What a nuisance this leaf money was. Just imagine stuffin' all those leaves in your back pocket!) In 1749 when the justices tried to sell the land and have the jail torn down, no one was interested. Finally, after some considerable time, Henry Jacobs "stole" the land for fifty pounds, not of tobacco leaves...they had been done away with by then. A house was built atop the old foundation. When the reconstruction of Queenstown took place, the foundation was unearthed and the courthouse rebuilt just as it was.

During those times, when Queenstown was growing and was the chief port on the Shore, she had the "distinction" of having the first legalized whipping post. Corporal punishment was the way and was enforced

27

at Gallows Field on the edge of town. Records show that in 1718 a Catherine Langton received ten lashes on her bare back, and that a man was branded with the code word cheat for reducing the peck measurement. The previously mentioned code was as follows: A seditious libeler, an S and L on either cheek; manslaughter, an M; thief, a T on the left hand; rape (oh yes, then too), an R on a shoulder (apparently it didn't matter which shoulder); and perjury, a P on the forehead. However inhumane this type of punishment seemed, it was the way of the day. This sort of brutality was eventually abandoned and fines as punishment became more prevalent. Today Queenstown is peaceful, a quiet place where you can hear the sound of a hummingbird's wings.

There was no Centreville when it was decided to move the county seat from Queenstown. Streets were named by the commissioners and lots laid out in one-half-acre sites. A jail was planned. The commissioners stated that the sheriff, whoever he be, was prohibited from keeping an "ordinary" or a house of "entertainment" at the jail. Swine were no longer allowed on the city streets, it was wisely decided.

"Modern" methods of agriculture were attempted, some startling. A try at growing Palmi Christi or castor oil beans was unsuccessful. Another entrepreneur planted mulberry trees on the south side of the Corsica River, and imported silkworms hoping that they would spin lots of strong silk in constructing their cocoon. The Mulberry Farm was a failure in terms of silk, (this silkworm scam in Queen Anne's was a spinoff from Talbot County, only on a smaller scale), but peaches flourished, and by 1875, there were one hundred and sixty-five thousand trees. Half of the fruit was canned on Mulberry Farm, whose name had changed to Royal Top Peach Farm. It was known as the largest peach farm in the world.

"King" tobacco had lost its crown and warehouses were closing. The General Assembly passed a law in which it was ordered that every tobacco farmer must plant at least two acres in corn. There was a fifty dollar fine for not complying.

Queen Anne's growth had a lot to do with transportation. The Queen Anne's Railroad was finished in 1868, and the first steamboat had already appeared in 1813. Lotteries are not new ways for states or counties to add revenue. They had lotteries in Queen Anne's County way back, and the funds supported the building of roads, bridges, schools, churches and ferries. Not many laborers were looking for employment, so the county court was petitioned to allow convicts to be brought over from across the Bay to provide workers for the plantations. This idea was not looked upon with favor, by most.

These were good times and leisure activities were paramount. Fox hunts, which had been put aside, became popular again. The first recorded hunt held in the New World was in the County in 1650. They hunted gray foxes at first, until a pair of red foxes jumped ship and settled in the County. A great ball was held to celebrate the arrival of this fine breed and the expected offspring. (Sort of like an Indian Rain Dance?) Every hunter of note had a slave to tend **only** to the hounds who chased the foxes. Queen Anne's County was the first to run organized horse races.

Now since you have maneuvered your way across the Kent Narrows Bridge and are on the mainland and have seen Queenstown and learned all about how Centreville came to be the county seat, you will come upon the Wye Mill Pond and the mill and the rest that is there, if you follow the signs.

The Wye Mill Pond freezes up in the winter and everyone used to get out and slide on their...whatever they could find. When your grandpa was a tadpole, folks pulled on their skates while sitting around the bonfire and then went skating or sliding on the stiff pond. The familiar nose-twisting smell of steaming wool toasted by the fire found its way up your frozen nose, and your fingers turned purple and hard with the bitter cold. You sat on a log and roasted marshmallows and toes at the same time. Trucks, owned by the tough and rough, were driven right out on the pond just to see if it could be done without cracking the ice and drowning yourself as well as the truck. (Boys will be boys.)

In the good ol' summertime, fishing was what you did on the pond. It was a delight then, when all you had to do was bait a hook with a fat slimy worm, and snag a carp, catfish, bass or a crappie. This pond feeds the old Wye Mill, and the stream forms the boundary between Talbot County and Queen Anne's.

A mill was the same as the general store. This mill has seen the goings-on in the County for over three hundred and some odd years. She has listened to talk of fox hunts, politics, seen cockfighting, heard the guns of war cracking and concealed a jug or two of moonshine, when it was necessary. (Which it always is, isn't it?) Today the mill is no longer another version of the general store as it was in days past, but a place where noisy groups of school kids point fingers at the grinding wheel, and tourists buy a poke of cornmeal to get the two recipes enclosed.

You could wile away a day (sorry trite, but right) in the small villages that surround Centreville. If you do, you might try Church Hill. The name, of course, came from St. Luke's Protestant Episcopal Church built in 1731. The church was built as a chapel of ease (easy to get to) to Old Chester Church. The reason to see this church is to read the two tablets presented by Queen Anne which have the Lord's Prayer and the Ten Commandments engraved in gold. The Methodists didn't rate such attention, since Queen Anne was an Episcopalian. The Methodists, however, built their church closer to the water. (Location! Location!) The Episcopal Church fell into ruins. (Remember there were few roads in those days. The byways of the day were the waterways.) Then the Methodists had the only place of worship until St. Luke's was renovated in the middle 1800s. The Methodists, whose membership grew rapidly in Queen Anne's as they had all over the Shore, built a fancy new edifice in 1857.

Church Hill once had a tavern and later a hotel and an enclosed commons where garden plots were available for anyone who wanted to grow vegetables, like in World War II when everyone had victory gardens.

You would have called Sudlersville, Sudler's Crossroads if you lived there in 1795. Then a forge mill was milling, and a warehouse and the well-known Dixon's Tavern thrived. Bog iron ore was a source of income. When the railroad came to town, the event was so momentous that it caused the name to be changed to Sudlersville and the crossroads became an enterprising place for a time.

"When people gather in the church, there is, for sure, good food." (So says the booklet that tells you about Queen Anne's.) "Church cookbooks are sourcebooks for the finest kitchens...good cooks love to share their favorite recipes among themselves, and the rest of us envy their culinary talents." This statement was made by the reverend of the Calvary-Asbury Methodist Church. He is speaking of the church cookbook which features recipes for dishes like Calico Beans, Hot Crab Pie and Crab Casserole. (In the event that the reader may not be able to get a copy of this publication, herein are the following selected recipes, selected by the author.)

Calico beans, "One tsp. salt, one tsp. dry mustard, two tsps. vinegar, one-half cup ketchup, three-quarter's cup brown sugar, one 16-oz. can baked beans, kidney beans, and butter beans, one-half pound bacon, and one pound hamburger. Fry the bacon, brown the hamburger, and add onion to your taste, and put it in a crock pot for five to six hours. Umm!

One more? Try this hot crab pie if you're a crab person. "One pound backfin, one-half bottle capers, one tsp. grated lemon peel, one-half tsp. Accent, dash of Tabasco, two cups mayonnaise, three-quarter's of a pound of grated sharp cheese and one Tbsp. horseradish. Mix it all up, but the cheese. Spread in a ten-inch glass pie plate and cover with the cheese. Bake at 350 degrees for twenty to thirty minutes and serve with crackers."

(The writer suspects that the reader might be upset by not including the one remaining recipe spoken of, so here it is.) Crab Casserole, "crabmeat, one pound, one-half cup of celery, chopped onions and green peppers, all combined with one-half cup of mayonnaise, salt and pepper, a dash of Worcestershire and a pinch of seafood seasoning. Put the mix in a casserole topped with seasoned croutons and butter, bake at 350 degrees for forty-five minutes." (Sounds perfectly marvelous!)

Millington, at the Head-of-Chester, borders Kent County and what little is left of the original town is there. The Queen Anne's County side of town burned in 1818 and a drive was made to rebuild, but the hamlet was never again the same.

In the northeast section of Queen Anne's was Hackett Sewell's General Store. In the Folk History of Queen Anne's County, published by the Queen Anne's County Record Observer/Kent Island Bay Times newspapers of Chesapeake Publishing Company, Alfred B. Covington tells A. C. Kidd how he remembers it.

"I remember when...Hackett Sewell's general store, located in the northeast corner of the intersection of the Centreville-Easton Road with the Wye Mills-Hillsboro Road, was many things to many people. The two-story building provided business space on the first floor and living quarters or storage space on the second floor. An uneven brick-floored porch extended across the front of the building. In good weather men occupied the benches placed there for their ease. From this vantage point anything of interest could be easily observed, participated in, or commented upon as suited the inclination of the individual.

"The reputation of this place of business was such that salesmen who served the area tried to make this their last call of the day so that they could spend as much time as possible enjoying the diversion or entertainment of the moment. The store was the scene of many practical jokes perpetrated by the owner, a forum for political discussions, a place to 'stretch the blanket' by tellers of tall tales, and community center, without having the formal designation, as well as existing for its intended purpose of selling general merchandise.

"Gas was the same price no matter who pumped it from its tank beside the road in front of the store. By moving a long lever back and forth gas was raised into a large glass globe bearing marks showing the number of gallons marked on the side, and then gravity took care of filling the vehicle's tank. Also located on this 'self service island' was 55-gallon drums of motor oil which could be drawn off a quart at a time and then added to the car. In early days oil was added almost as often as gas.

"With a basket of eggs or some poultry many a farmer exchanged his bounty for items not produced at home choosing from foodstuffs, shoes, overalls, plows, plants.

"At the far end of the store past the wheel of sharp cheese (for the owner's cat and customers), past the half bushel bag of peanuts (where a rat trap was once set to discourage a salesman from helping himself), past the big stove where men sat comfortably tilted back in their chairs (unless sneezing from heated black pepper casually blown from the stove in their direction), past the large glass display cases set on the wooden counters one arrived at the communications center (also known as the telephone). Long before answering services became part of our lives, Sewell provided this service for his regular customers, and there were many. There was no charge for this as it was part of being open for business and the convenience of his customers.

"One day Buddy Callahan, a regular, parked his brakeless car against a hitching post and returned to find that the car could not be backed away from the post despite the help of several husky men pushing it. Investigation showed that the car's front axle had been chained to the post. Callahan claimed the new chain as his own; and the prankster, participants and onlookers had their laughs.

"Another man who carefully secreted his whiskey (carried in a vinegar bottle) outside the building found, on taking his next swig, that it had been replaced by a vinegar bottle containing the real thing.

"Inside, a man napping on the counter was provided with wake-up services when a mouse was let loose to run up his pant leg.

"Until shortly after the death of the postmaster, Mr. John B. T. Roe, in 1934 the post office occupied the right front side of the building.

"Before Christmas one of the store's big windows would be divided into many sections which were then filled with various unwrapped candy and unshelled nuts in a convenient display for sampling and sales.

"In the 1930s the store was the scene of nightly checker games with Harry Denny, Don Rathell, Stanley Walker and this teller of tales being acknowledged as the pros. In Hillsboro or at Willoughby in Winnie Smith's General Store this group could hold their own, but no one could 'get to the king row' when they played with the real professionals at Callahan's Hardware Store in Centreville.

"Hackett Sewell's store may have been one of a kind in this land of pleasant living in the good old days."

Besides general stores, taverns were another place where the "guys" hung out. Crumpton was not far from where the general store was once, and there were several places of congeniality in town. The Blazing Bay, Little Hill in the Hollow and the Do Drop Inn were the favorites. There was something, however, that no general store or tavern could offer in the way of entertainment, and that was live theater. There were stock companies putting on "Uncle Tom's Cabin" and "Ten Nights in a Barroom" in Centreville's "Opera House," and concerts on the green, but that was in Centreville, the county seat, and this was Crumpton way up on the Chester River just across from Kent County.

But Crumpton did have the wonderful floating playhouse. When she arrived at Picnic Point, signs would go up in store windows telling folks that the James Adams Floating Theater was coming to spend a week. Besides the signs in the windows, the theater's orchestra boarded small boats and played their way up and down the inlets and creeks blasting out the message that the playhouse had arrived. Their music was "unique" and thought by some to be kind 'a kooky.

Everyone was spellbound by the idea of the theater. It was Broadway, it was splashy, it was the biggest event of the year. On Sunday afternoons, when the showboat was expected, the wharf at Crumpton was jammed up with all the folks in town waiting for the "steamboat" to round the bend. When the whistles blasted, everyone screamed and yelled, "Here she comes!" The wharf trembled as hands waved and daddies held their kids on their shoulders so they could see. Big ropes were thrown out and tied to the pilings and folks crowded aboard to buy tickets to the show.

Of all the elegant steamers who docked along the Shore, none was looked forward to more than the James Adams Floating Theater. The official name was "Playhouse," and she wasn't a steamboat. She wasn't even attractive on the outside like the steamboats, but beauty is in the eyes of the beholder.

The floating theater was a "hulk" measuring one hundred twenty-eight feet in length and thirty-four in beam, and drew only fourteen inches of water; her bottom was flat as a pancake. The Elk and the Trouper, two tugs, pulled her along. Inside she was a different lady. She could seat seven hundred, had eight combination dressing room--bedrooms behind the nineteen-foot wide stage. Aft there was a dining room for the actors who traveled with the "ship." Her seats were plush, both in fabric and appearance, and comfy as Morris chairs. She was one in a million, one of a kind, there were none like her on the Bay. She brought with her the magic of make-believe.

Every night was a different show. During intermission, after the main show, boxes of candy kisses, with prizes inside, were peddled for 25 cents. The stage was brilliant with colored lights. The actors, the crew and the musicians mingled with the great crowds of patrons who came from all over, in a way "stars" seldom do. Everyone felt special when they could touch a real live "star."

The shows began at 8:15 p.m. and 10:15 p.m. There was a concert and vaudeville acts which cost an extra 10 or 15 cents. The Saturday matinee always had different acts, **always**. They did not perform on Sunday.

You could buy your ticket, though. The actors were versatile and performed mostly three-act plays like, "Big Shot," "Breakfast for Two" (not to be confused with "Breakfast at Tiffany's"), "Tempest," "Sunshine," "Frisa," "Jemme" and "Man's Will, Woman's Way." (The last one wouldn't be so popular today.)

The star was Adams' daughter, who had a number of different leading men, finally married one, and he became the permanent leading man. She was thought of as the "Mary Pickford of the Chesapeake." Edna Ferber, of popular acclaim, came aboard and spent a week to work on her book, Show Boat, later filmed at Crumpton.

Things went along just fine, until one night the Corsica River rose so high, in a nor'easter, that when the show was over there was nearly two feet of water over the wharf. Well, the able-bodied men gallantly turned up their pant legs and carried all the ladies to safety on the shore. The playhouse sank twice and was refloated and renovated. Finally a fire took her and she sank to the bottom of the Chesapeake Bay.

Around the time the floating theater was losing out to the changing country, the Chautauqua came and combined their moral message and self-improvement hints with good times in a way only the Methodists can do. They held their show in tents. The talent was excellent, everyone agreed. There were musicians and magicians and lectures were given. William Jennings Bryan's "Cross of Gold" and Russell Cornwall's "Acres of Diamonds" were hits always. Later they put on three-day programs in the Opera House. The Chautauqua began in Upper New York State in 1874 as a series of Methodist Bible classes, meetings, and expanded to become a national lecture and entertainment organization that toured the country.

Looking down the Chester River from the place where the playhouse docked, there is nothing to see except in your mind's eye. If night's darkness has not come and you imagine, maybe you will see Henry McCallister pulling his rope raft across the river. Crumpton was the "owner" of the town, and McCallister had the ferry.

Crumpton was a "planned" city, like so many on the Shore. The plans included one-and-one-half square miles laid out in blocks with the streets running parallel to the river and avenues crossing. The assessed value of an acre was twenty-seven shillings then. (The author cannot convert English shillings into American bills, but be sure it was a bargain if compared to today's prices for land.)

There were **fourteen** general stores across the river. There are no stores today and no sign of any having ever existed on the Kent County side of the river. McCallister's ferry took folks across to grocery shop until a drawbridge was built. These were good times in Crumpton. Then the railroad abandoned its building along with the B. S. Ford steamboat, which it also owned. The steamboat was junked and the building left to the ravages of time. In 1961 a concrete span was built across the river. There was a parade and a celebration with Governor Theodore McKeldin giving the dedication speech.

Today there are some large Victorian homes in Crumpton, but not much else. Along the lovely Chester River where the James Adams Floating Theater docked and folks watched her round the bend calling out, "There she comes," only crumbling hunks of concrete hidden in the tall grasses give evidence that the playhouse once landed at Crumpton.

Another kind of "show" has replaced those put on by the floating theater. The largest auction on the Eastern Shore takes place every Wednesday at Crumpton. Locals, in particular, look forward to Wednesday when the sale is like old home week. (Sorry trite, but right.) They meet their friends and browse around, looking over everything and anything anyone could possibly imagine. (Good Pennsylvania Dutch food, too!)

The Corsica River has only five miles to flow before she slips into the Chesapeake Bay. Along those five miles the river has cut steep banks that cover their nakedness with thick stands of woods. If you spread the foliage with your fingers and peek through, you will see the fertile farms of Queen Anne's County, their fields green with life.

Centreville is small-town USA. You will have no doubt about it when you park your car on **Liberty** Street and put a nickel in the true blue parking meters or when you amble past the barber pole or when you see the clock, with hands which seem two feet long, on top of the building on the corner of Lawyers Row, no doubt about it!

Stately trees shade pathways that meander through the green grass in front of the courthouse. Splashes of pink and purple, gold, red and orange flowers brighten the scene. On any weekday in the summertime, you will see the courtyard filled with the brown-bag-for-lunch-bunch who, leading the leisurely life, spend their noontime in this bower of serenity, presided over by an imposing statue of Queen Anne. The attractive young lady perched on a throne bears no resemblance to the Queen, a stout (a nice way of saying fat) ruler, who gave birth to seventeen children.

The Queen Anne's County Courthouse, 1791, is one of two original courthouses in continuous use in the state of Maryland. The hip-roofed center section is decorated with an ornate balcony, added in the nineteenth century. The rich whipped cream color of the painted brick is a change from the usual red brick courthouses on the Shore, but a nice one. The iron balcony protects the double front doors which are presided over by the American bald eagle. (Again small-town patriotism is reflected in this symbol of our country.) The trim is a soft slate blue and with the arched windows and the balcony, you feel an antebellum ambiance, a sense of the Deep South, which extends to the homes in town with porches and backyard flower gardens.

The Wright's Chance House was moved to town from a plantation and is the home of the Historical Society, which has tastefully restored it. The wood paneling is original and most of the windows are that wavy glass which was the best obtainable in those days. The gardens in the rear are "done" in boxwood and exude that sweet pungent odor so familiar in the older homes all over Maryland. The old trees would be delighted to provide shade for your tea party, if you lived there.

It is a pleasant meander into yesterday on the tree shaded streets of Centreville.

Tucker House, possibly the oldest in Centreville, stands on a lot purchased by Elizabeth Nicholson from James Kennard in 1792. The house is a "living" museum with photos, old documents and scrapbooks which detail Queen Anne's County's eighteenth century homes and buildings.

Centreville's street names like **Bayou Lane** and **Happy Lady Lane,** can't help but make you smile at what some might label quaint, but are really simply unique.

Fortunately, the Tucker House was further south on Commerce Street when the fire of December 4, 1902, burned down most of the business district. It was early, about 4 a.m., when some cardboard boxes, stored in the cellar of a structure on the southwest corner of Commerce and Lawyers Row, ignited.

The word went out! The fire company assembled! Horses pulled up the "pumper!" "Turn on the water!" No water! Incinerated was most of Lawyers Row and a good deal of Commerce Street.

That night folks were aroused from their sleep by the mouthwatering aroma of roasted potatoes. It seems that the railroad agent had a sideline, growing potatoes. His field had been harvested and the spuds were stored in the basement of Al Green's Store. It took a week before they cooled down. Everyone joked about the hot potatoes that weren't stuffed, nor buttered, nor edible, but smelled good!

During the fire, a salvage operation by the ladies in town was attempted. They grabbed the hems of those long white aprons everyone wore, and carried merchandise in the "basket" formed by the cotton cloth. It was Christmastime, and their valiant attempt to save enough of the Christmas items, so at least the children could have presents, failed. It was a bleak Christmas that year.

If you lived in Centreville then, you might have taken your fishing pole down to the wharf, where the

43

packing houses were, or to the catfish hole back of Wes Thompson's home. If you caught a mess you took them to Mr. Swenkey's, a shanty with a curtain to close off the sleeping area for his dog Fannie and himself, and the rest was only a chair, table, stove, water bucket and wash basin. He was comfortable. He never complained. If you hooked four or five catfish, you hoped Mr. Swenkey would scrub 'em up, flour and fry 'em nice and brown and crisp for you. He usually did. Or you could doze a bit in the sun and just watch the double-masted schooners, the work horses of that day, loading goods and produce for delivery to and from the Eastern Shore. They docked in front of what was called, the "JUMBO" Building, no one knows exactly why, except that it was a big barn-like structure.

The fourth of July was always celebrated at the wharf. Your papa would treat the family to ice cream from the ice packing house, and your mom fried chicken. The lunch basket was put in the boat decorated with an American flag to honor the day. You met your fellow or gal after the parade and hung around together waiting for the fireworks. The sky rockets were always the best and saved for last. They lit the sky as bright as any October moon. It was all over then, and you started looking forward to next year.

Saturday night you probably went to the Opera House where a roving troop of troubadours entertained. If it was really important, like your high school graduation or a fancy banquet, you held the affair at the armory. Now the vacant building only echoes the sounds of martial music and the laughter of those days long gone.

Centreville was queen for a day when Princess Anne came to visit. In June of 1977 the residents were propelled into activity with the announcement of the arrival of royalty. The princess sailed across the sea to deliver the bronze statue of Queen Anne, who now presides over the "doings" at the courthouse. The royal Princess arrived with Captain Mark Phillips. The fanfare was unequaled in the County since her founding two hundred and seventy-one years before. Centreville was awash with Union Jacks fluttering like seas of marsh grass. The Princess smiled in her royal way, looking

44

cool in an apple green knit maternity dress. She was struck, she said, "by how the people of Queen Anne's County have managed to find a happy medium of being able to live efficiently in this energetic County and still have time for each other...a place where roots go deep." Blair Lee, the acting Governor at that time, shook hands with the Princess. Everyone took pictures and the town's clock chimed a welcome.

There was a parade of yachts unlike any you ever saw. The governor's yacht, filled with dignitaries, of course, led. The <u>Lady Maryland</u> was followed by other sumptuous yachts, motorboats and any and every kind of craft. The Bay work boats, contrasting rather sharply with the elegant sailboats, brought up the rear. No one cared. After all the work boats were one of the reasons everyone was on the Eastern Shore.

All over the County there were celebrations, jousting tournaments (the state of Maryland's official sport), an Invitational Horse Show, the Stadium Jumping Event and a display of dressage where horses showed off their skills. Flags flew, folks partied and picnicked, and during all of these goings-on, the Princess waved and smiled as she was accustomed to doing. All had a fine time, as will you, in Queen Anne's County. There is something fetching about the County, and if you will allow, she will bestow on you the gift of "logical stillness" (T. S. Elliot).

USEFUL INFORMATION

Queen Anne's County Courthouse at Queenstown, Route 18, off US 301, Queenstown. Tours by appointment. Open on Queen Anne's Day.

Tucker House, 124 South Commerce Street, Centreville. May-October, 12:30-3:30pm. Winter, Fridays, 11am-4pm.

Wright's Choice (Museum of Queen Anne's Historical Society), 119 South Commerce Street, Centreville. May-October, Fridays, 12:30-3:30pm.

For information and guides write: Tourism Council of the Upper Chesapeake, P.O. Box 66, Centreville, Maryland 21617.

TALBOT COUNTY

THE COLONIAL CAPITAL COUNTY

TALBOT COUNTY

Talbot County, pronounced Tall-bot, is the answer to one's dreams, the locals tell you. If being where you are surrounded by six hundred miles of shoreline, if living where you can net crabs in your backyard, if living where history comes to life in towns like St. Michaels and Oxford is your dream, then Talbot County is for you.

Talbot County is old; her history goes back to 1661 when the colony was named after the third Lord Baltimore's sister, Grace Talbot. Originally Talbot County embraced an area including all of what is now Queen Anne's County, except for Kent Island, part of today's Kent County, and the northern half of Caroline County. All of this land was a grant to Charles Calvert by the first Lord Baltimore.

This land grant was a long time ago and things and places and names and events are often forgotten as though they had never been, like ghost towns. When you think of ghost towns, generally the image is of a once flourishing settlement in the Wild West with a saloon, a pokey and hitching posts, filled with cowboys and settlers in covered wagons. Those towns are still there for you to see, unlike the four ghost towns of Talbot County that cannot even be located, let alone seen.

Colonial Courthouse At York

You will not find York on today's state map. In fact, you cannot even find the early settlement located somewhere along the banks of Skipton Creek. Old York blossomed in 1681 and wilted in 1710. York had highfalutin ideas of becoming the county seat; no one had heard of Easton. Back then, Talbot County was larger and hard to govern. Getting around in the, then, wilderness was a chore and because there was no official county seat, court was held in people's homes. The far-flung front room courts held session in places as far north as the Chester River. Galloping around on horseback through the virgin forests caused the judges pain and suffering from carbuncles and calluses and they rebelled, demanding a centrally-located place of government. Land along the Wye River was selected to build a courthouse.

No one knows for sure if a building was ever constructed, or if the court was actually held in a tavern owned by Jonathan Hopkinson, a structure that already existed. The records are so confusing and conflicting only those who kept them could explain the meaning, and one doubts that even they could. Evidently the area had no name until the General Assembly, in St. Mary's City, selected York. It is supposed that the court was held in the tavern because an old court order stated, "no drink be sold or consumed when the court is in session."

It is certain that in 1879 a contract was let to erect a courthouse on the County's land at Wye. For its time, this three-story structure was unusual since most were a story and a half at best.

A small settlement grew around this, then, Port of Entry. The courthouse was "sole source" of entertainment and alcoholic beverages. A "boom" town was born when a mill, a tobacco warehouse or two and the only measured race track around was built. This half mile track was the first of many to come in Maryland. (As I am sure you are aware.)

Shore folks flocked to the track to wager and tipple and generally become unruly. The situation grew grim when a group headed by Reverend John Lillingston, rector of Old Wye Church, a chapel of ease for St.

51

Paul's Parish, took rooms in the tavern. The reverend and his associates were disposed to take exception with the political views of those in power down in St. Mary's City. They got into a chug-a-lug contest, so to speak, and to ridicule the court, and as a way to blow off steam (sorry trite, but right), they rode their horses into the courtroom and tied the reins to the judge's bench. That did it! The judge was not pleased and, as was within his power, the reverend and his companions were put in the pokey. Even though they were guilty, the men were released before finishing their sentences "on account of His Majesty's happy success, and later victory, against the French."

Things were going pretty well at the Port of Entry until the General Assembly established a new county lying between the Chester and Wye Rivers. Queen Anne's was born in 1706 and York was no longer in the center of things, both actually and factually. York was then on the northern border of the new county. Lovely Oxford was selected and the last session of the court was held in York on August 21, 1706.

In spite of the Port of Entry and the tobacco barn and the mill and the people and the race track, old York simply became a ghost of a town vanishing as if it had never been. York has no marker to prove its existence, only a few sunken places thought to be the cellars on which houses once stood.

Doncaster or Wye Town, on the banks of the Wye River, was an important center of commerce. (This Doncaster is not the present day city of Doncaster on the Miles River. Just want to make that clear.) A valiant effort was made to persuade those in power that Doncaster should be the county seat. Doncaster may have been the center of commerce, but was not in the center of the new county either. Regardless, the authorities were petitioned asking that the seat of government be Doncaster. But no! The honor went to Oxford.

Some say there was a town, and to prove it, an antiquarian went to the supposed site of the ghost town to see what he could dig up. After lots of walking in the weeds and underbrush along the Wye and splashing around in the marshes, he was rewarded when he located, under lots of slime and mud, the gravestone of the High Sheriff of Talbot County, Francis Butler, who drowned in 1689.

Oxford, such a favorite at first, held court for three years, again, in folks' homes. One major reason Oxford did not remain the county seat was the wood-eating bore that infected the waters of the Tred Avon and caused the disappearance of the shipping trade. No courthouse was ever built. Oxford really wasn't, really, in the center of the new county, even though chosen by the Assembly.

Kingstown, the least known of Talbot's ghost towns, was located at King's Creek, a tributary of the Choptank River. Everyone who owned plantations, and most did, needed a settlement and through the good graces of Lord Baltimore, that need was filled. The Act of 1669 established Kingstown by name, but not much happened. The fresh water of the Choptank, where Kingstown was supposedly located, was free of the dreaded boring worms who had infected the Tred Avon River. At least Kingstown was mentioned in a number of documents and was a port of entry, even shown on the state map as late as 1961, long after York had disappeared. All of the steamboat lines serving the area noted Kingstown as a stop in their records from 1870 to the 1900s. Apparently that was all Kingstown ever was. If there was a settlement, it vanished into time.

Lord Baltimore, in an attempt to increase revenue to the Crown, designated certain places within the new county as ports. Dover was one of those lucky ones. Dover, which had only a ferry across the Choptank River, was now a port! But, where was Dover...on the main road from Oxford, or the road to the Trappe area, or on the road to Talbot Courthouse (an early name for Easton)? No one knows for sure. These three roads still exist but no longer converge. As late as 1917 a tiny graveyard where Dover might have existed along the Choptank River has an unnerving, disturbing, winged-skull tombstone.

Reverend Thomas Bacon, pastor of White Marsh Church and founder of the first free school in Talbot,

noted the number of transfers of goods taking place at Dover--meaning that there must have been landings and quays available. There was a record of judgment against a Deborah Nichols for not having kept the ferry going when she was supposed to. She was to have her allowance (another word for pay) cut in half the next year if the ferry didn't operate as scheduled. The ferry was poorly located anyway, and before long was moved two miles up and to the other side of the Choptank where the river was narrower, making the crossing shorter.

While those in the place called Talbot Town, near Pitt's Bridge, were busy building a thriving community, folks connected with the government were moving in, the go-getters from Dover got going and snuck up to Annapolis, by then the capital city of Maryland. They were successful in getting the General Assembly to agree to introduce this measure, "That the Judges of the General Court, or any one of them, shall hold their first Court for the transacting and determining the business of the Eastern Shore at Talbot Courthouse, in Talbot County, on the second Tuesday of September next, and on the second Tuesday of April and September, until a town shall be laid out in Dover, and a Court and prison there erected, after which the said Court for the Eastern Shore shall be forever held at Dover on the second Tuesday of April and September." There you have it. What a coup.

Nobody's fool, these Talbotian townsmen went to work and in December 1785 a measure to get their town on record was introduced. An act passed on March 12, 1786, creating a town with definite boundaries, laid out in streets, squares and "public grounds" and named Talbot Town. To be sure, another bill was passed providing that the judges of the General Court shall hold their courts to determine business of Maryland's Eastern Shore at Talbot, in Talbot County, and the name of the town will be Easton. This was how Easton began.

Besides ghost towns, ghosts and spooks are haunting houses which **can** still be located in Talbot County. Outside of Easton, Gross Coate, the ancestral home of the Tilghman family from 1760 until 1983, is "occupied" by Aunt Molly, a spirit who in life, in the 1700s, lived there with her brother, Richard, and his family.   Richard, being prominent and moneyed, commissioned Charles Wilson Peale, the well-known painter, to execute portraits of several family members.

Peale was a widower in his late forties with several children, and deeply in debt. He asked for Molly's hand in marriage. Her brother, Richard, was scandalized by this proposal from a much older man and sent Peale packing. Peale returned to Philadelphia where he had a museum displaying, among other things, a three-legged cow with two tails.

Over the years Molly grew fond of a ne'er-do-well nephew who came to live with her. She would wait up at night for his return from carousing around the countryside. The tap, tap, of her cane on the steps as she came down to unlock the front door, can still be heard. Folks claim they have caught glimpses of this ghostly apparition pacing from room to room waiting for her errant nephew.

Fairview, a yellow brick mansion, was a land grant from Lord Baltimore in 1633. The boxwood gardens, considered fine enough to have the small estate included in the Maryland House and Garden Pilgrimage, are haunted! Strange noises, whispers, from one ghost to another, have been reported. Down along the Miles River a Tory still waits to guide British warships to St. Michaels for the attack during the Revolutionary War. The apparition is a ghostly rider who gallops madly down the road along the river, barely missing the branches of the trees in his mad race to nowhere, causing a ruckus and disturbing the peaceful reverie of those who tread the path.

Not only along the river and in the garden, but the mansion is also haunted, by Alicia Lloyd, a great beauty, whose body is buried in the family graveyard on the estate, but whose soul rests by the fireplace in the drawing room. The current owner attests to having seen the old woman wearing a gray bonnet, hands folded in her lap, rocking continually back and forth, back and forth, waiting for something to happen, but nothing ever does.

Even in Talbot County the bulldozer tears the land as inevitable "progress" intrudes. Left behind by the

56

shovel of these monster machines was a human skeleton, a skull and a jawbone. Alerted to this unseemly display, the state had the remains interred, believed to be those of Captain Fairbanks.

Captain Fairbanks' ghost has been "living" in the house on Indian Point for some time. His slippered feet tread the floors as he "plays" with the appliances. Seemingly fascinated with the modern world, he likes to turn on the dishwasher, the fan above the electric stove, switch the lights on and off, and, when bored, move the furniture in the two upstairs bedrooms to suit himself.

Being a friendly sort of ghost, he tried to climb in bed with the owner who swears she could see the indentation of his body beside her. Although a nuisance, the captain has been welcome ever since he caused the owner to awaken early one morning, even though she didn't smell smoke, and go downstairs to find the fireplace ablaze.

Here's another one about a ghoul, two ghouls really, who dug up corpses looking for valuables. Reverend Maynadier, the rector of White Marsh Church in 1771, honored his wife's dying wish, to be buried with a valuable family ring on her finger. Grave robbers often attended funerals hoping to catch a glimpse of the corpse, sort of "casing" the situation, to see if there was anything worth stealing before going to the grave to dig up the dearly departed. These two were no exception.

To remove a ring from a stiff "stiff's" finger required the removal of the digit. Fresh air rushed into the coffin as the blade pierced Mrs. Maynadier's joint. She screamed and sat up, suddenly restored to the land of the living. The reprobates froze, galvanized by the specter, then fled no one knows where.

The reverend's wife was somewhat disheveled from climbing out of the dirt-filled grave and a bit delirious from the shock of this life after death experience, but managed to run all the way to the parsonage, where she collapsed on the front stoop. The reverend, deeply saddened by his wife's demise, was staring at the flames burning in the fireplace when he heard her wailing. He sprang for the door and carried his shrouded wife's body inside. They both lived many years and when the grim reaper came, this time she went and so did he. They are buried side by side in White Marsh Cemetery.

White Marsh Church is in ruins. Today only the graveyard remains--a reminder of those who worshipped there so long ago. If you venture in among the graves, you may hear someone whisper in a tortured voice, "Oh show me the way." If this apparition speaks to you, you are to say, "Too late, it is too late. Yes, doctor, it is too late! I have just come from there and he died two hours ago, bled to death. You could have helped him had you arrived last night."

The voice will begin again, "Show me the way." And again you answer, "It is too late." If you get tired of this conversation with a spook, you might look for, but you won't find, where the good folk of Easton buried the doctor which had only the words, "Rest in Peace" engraved on the stone.

A piece about this ghost, who lived so long ago, ran in the Baltimore Sun Newspaper, October 31, 1972. (Halloween, I believe.) What happened was the "good" doctor was into his cups pretty heavily the night he got the call (not by phone) to come to the bedside of his very good friend who had shot himself. The doctor was barely able to stand, let alone handle the wheel (excuse me...reins) of his steed and guide the carriage through the heavy snow. He raced around the countryside calling out, "Show me the way! Show me the way!" He dozed off, and the next day the buggy and the doctor's dead body were found under a bridge, gone but not forgotten.

White Marsh Cemetery is very visible from Route 50, east of Easton, but my guess is you have never noticed it. Still standing in a grove of locust trees are the jagged remains of the church's red brick front wall with the arched entrance gaping open, the brick floor is intact, and in the rear, the old brick altar could be used today. That is all though, no other walls nor roof. Just outside the section of wall is the raised grave of Robert Morris, Sr. A rather lengthy

inscription on the flat concrete cover is still readable (only because it has been restored). The entrance to the cemetery is through two brick pillars onto a rut cut by a car's wheels. The trail leads past a surprising number of twentieth century marble markers to the grove of trees where the old stones are tilted and toppled and most inscriptions unreadable. It must be there, the graves of the Reverend Maynadier and his wife, and the doctor, but where? (Under the brick floor.)

If you can imagine what this small church might have looked like a couple hundred years ago, then perhaps you can visualize Tench Francis Tilghman's marriage to Elizabeth Turbutt. Tench Francis Tilghman, grandfather of the Revolutionary War hero, Tench Tilghman, and of Peggy Shippens who married Benedict Arnold, eloped with Elizabeth. Because, of course, her family objected to a union with Tench Francis who then was only a law student. The men of the Turbutt family dashed after the couple and got to the church just as the minister was saying, "If any man hath just cause to forbid this marriage..." Before a word could be spoken, Tench Francis drew his sword and declared, "If any man gainsayeth this marriage I will run him through with my sword!" That settled it, and the two were married.

Chaucer's "Canterbury Tales," like the tall tales of Canterbury House, would fill a book and did once, but not with haunts. Canterbury House has loads of ghosts. The old place was once a British jail house. Recently some archaeologists dug up a skeleton shackled in manacles standing upright in a grave. The vertical position was intended to keep the soul from getting any sort of rest in heaven.

This discovery prompted further investigation, and a clairvoyant was called in to speak with the spirits suspected of inhabiting the house. Immediately upon entering the psychic broke out in goose bumps, a sure sign that something was amiss. Among her sightings was a tall pale woman who was later identified as a former owner. All that could be done was to tell the owner that Canterbury House was riddled with ghosts and that there were images of fires burning. Sure as shooting (sorry trite, but right), the oak tree in the yard broke into flames. Not long after, the owner's friend's home in Annapolis burned down.

Of all the spooks in Talbot County, the "Kissing Phantom of Trappe" is the best liked. He comes to your bedroom at night, if you are a lady, while you are sleeping, and bestows on you a mustachioed smacker, no more. Most of the ghosts predate a revolution which began in Talbot County almost ten years before the American Revolution.

On March 25, 1765, the County's freemen gathered on the courthouse grounds and hung a wooden effigy of a British tax informer. They resolved, "at the risk of our lives and fortunes, to take whatever lawful action should prove necessary against taxation by the British Government."

The hated Stamp Act required legal documents of all kinds, including newspapers and advertisements, be on special stamped paper which could be obtained only from agents of the British Crown. The Americans held, that since they had no representative in Parliament, this was taxation without representation.

On August 18, 1765, Jeremiah Banning, in command of the Layton, arrived at Oxford and was put-upon by a mob outraged over the presence of one of the passengers. They yelled, "Have you got Zachariah Hood on the ship?" The captain told the ugly mob that if he had known who the tax collector was, he would not have let him aboard. Hood was almost lynched, but managed to escape to Annapolis where he was not well received. Another effigy was hung and set afire by the furious residents. Zachariah Hood was a stubborn man who didn't know when he had worn out his welcome, but did know enough to flee Annapolis. In New York City, his last stop, he was "persuaded" to resign by The Sons of Liberty.

By the late 1700s things had quieted down and Talbot was an attractive place to live. In Easton the first theater on the Shore, The Maryland Company of Players, opened in "A Bold Stroke For A Wife." A dancing master offered "elegance and grace in movement and attitude" in his classes. A ballroom was built that hosted Washington's birthday balls and splashy events

of all kinds. The local newspaper took a dim view and blasted this frivolity saying that folks would give money for dances, but not a red cent (sorry trite, but right) to build a new church. One church held a lottery and one even built a race track the parishioners could attend after service. The lottery, to build a firehouse, did not do well and no one, apparently, cared if the public wharf was completed. There is no evidence of those "good old days" today.

The high-water mark for Talbot County was before and during the War of 1812. These were years of prosperity, towns sprung up everywhere, crops like corn, wheat and grains were sold to Europe at prices which made the farmers rich. Merchants moved in to help the farmers spend their new-found wealth. Shipbuilding in towns like Oxford and St. Michaels recorded all-time highs in employment. Immigrants, mostly Irish or Scotch carpenters, iron workers or shipbuilders, the sort who worked hard and played hard, moved in. As wickedness abounded, the courts were flooded with misdemeanor charges.

All this changed when Joseph Cromwell, the first Methodist to preach a sermon in Talbot County, arrived on his horse. Cromwell was a circuit riding parson who, like Joshua Thomas in Somerset County, saved souls in droves. Illiterate, but eloquent, he could preach the devil into Heaven, it was said. He was followed by Freeborn Garrettson, a highly literate and cultured man, who when he arrived in St. Michaels, said, and these are his words, "labored for two weeks, night and day, with tears." He set folks "at liberty" all over Talbot County.

The first tent camps were set up at the town of Wye in the summer of 1807, and thousands attended the camp meetings, common all over the Shore in those days. Hallelujahs were shouted so loud they could be heard for three miles. Eight thousand attended, like the multitudes of biblical times, the frenzy was overwhelming and most were reborn as Methodists, known today as "covered dishers," because of all the religious groups, the Methodists have the most potluck suppers. (Joke!)

Oh it was a high ol' time until after the War of 1812 when, like the Great Depression of the 1930s, everything crashed. The wars in Europe were ended and the soldiers became farmers and grew their own grain and didn't need to buy America's grain anymore, or anything else of consequence. Everyone went under (bankrupt) and the pickin's were slim. (Sorry trite, but right.) In times like these people snatched at straws (sorry trite, but right). Scams of one kind or another were given consideration, but two massive rip-offs, which bordered on the absurd, showed how gullible folks can be.

The Black Cat Fur Farm (don't laugh, it's true) was one of them. In Talbot County R. O. Ridgeway advertised that he would pay 25 cents each for a black female cat when delivered to Poplar Island. Ridgeway was the front man for Charles Carroll, grandson of the signer of the Declaration of Independence. Carroll, who owned the island, planned to fatten the felines with fish, let them carouse around the island which was far enough off shore so the kitty cats couldn't escape and then, when there were enough, they would be butchered and their skins sold to China. A large supply of black cats were enjoying the high ol' life (sorry trite, but right) with the toms who were already installed on the island. All cats involved in this "breeding" attempt had to be black because the market Carroll had heard of in China required black fur only. One dark winter night it was so cold that the water, between the mainland and the island, froze stiff and all the cats scurried ashore putting the Black Cat Fur Farm out of business. The fur farm shut down leaving Talbot County with a surplus of black cats which are still around.

The above **can** be topped by the silkworm swindle. It seems that fine silk was in great demand, no synthetic fabrics then, and Morus Multicaulis seedlings were imported from the South Seas. Yes, the South Seas! Folks actually demanded to be sold these Mulberry tree shoots. The idea was to grow a Mulberry tree, install a silkworm who would eat the leaves and form a cocoon, the fibers of which would be spun into fine silk, a cloth literally worth its weight in gold (sorry trite, but right) and everyone would join the ranks of the rich and famous. Every available plot of land was planted, with folks even mortgaging their property to get money to buy more seedlings. Mulberry trees began to rise from the soil and everyone waited with anticipation for the cocoons that were to be put in the trees. A cocoonery was open in Easton and situated at what came to be called, aptly enough, Mulberry Hill. The cocoonery didn't do much cocooning, but did sell seedlings, seedlings, seedlings.

The local paper estimated that one hundred thousand seedlings were planted within a mile of Easton. Everyone sat back and waited for the process to work. The fly in the pie (sorry trite, but right) proved to be a wrinkle not mentioned by the sellers of seedlings, that one had to be highly skilled with years of training to extract the fibers needed to spin silk from the cocoon. One wonders where all the Mulberry trees have gone. The truth is the seedlings were all yanked out of the ground to make room for paying crops.

One more try at easy money was made with the proposition to build a railroad down the center of the Delmarva Peninsula linking the prosperous cities in the north with the Cotton Belt in the south. The Baltimore, Wilmington and Philadelphia Line was funded and had started construction when the folks in Talbot County brainstormed this idea. The state of Maryland should pay for the railroad, hadn't they spent millions on canals and railroads for the "Western Shore?" Yes, they had, but they were conned into spending more, and in 1833 voted one million dollars in a capital stock grant to the Eastern Shore Railroad.

Lots of speculators bought in and the company was founded. Marketing con men knocked out a brochure telling tall tales of how fifty to sixty thousand people a year would travel from Charlotte and Savannah to New York and Boston by rail. There would be less track to lay than on the "other side," since the distance was shorter, and the train would be cheaper to build and operate, were some of the features in the brochure. Unfortunately, a nationwide collapse occurred, the depression of 1837, and capital dried up. It was fated to fail from the beginning because the bankers on the "Western Shore" saw no reason to build a railroad on the "other side" at the expense of their own areas. In spite of this gloom and doom, General Tench Tilghman, grandson of the hero of the Revolutionary War, broke ground for the eastern branch of the proposed railroad. The deep hole in the ground remained until after the Civil War.

Somewhat embittered by the attitude of the "Western Shore," it was decided to secede from the Union and become the new state of Delmarva, joining with Delaware and Virginia. They were serious about this in Talbot County. The measure had been raised in the State Legislature in 1833, but was put to death in the Senate by only a margin of five to four! In 1842 and 1850 these radical ideas came up again and each time it was voted down by western legislatures. They were still at it in 1949 when a letter, in the <u>Baltimore Sun Newspaper</u>, suggested that instead of building the Chesapeake Bay Bridge, the state should just give the Eastern Shore to Delaware and save fifty million dollars.

Once you cross the Bay Bridge and enter Talbot County, on Route 50, "Wye" not stop and see the ancient Wye Oak tree. This magnificent lady has a waistline of twenty-one feet and has been holding her one hundred sixty-five foot limbs up to God for almost four hundred years. In her bare feet she stands ninety-five feet tall. She is honored by being named the official Maryland State Tree. The Wye Oak is the oldest tree in the state and probably in America. She grows on one-and-one-half acres, surrounded by a white rail fence, in the smallest state park in Maryland. Children call the old oak awesome.

Nearby is the one-room schoolhouse, called the "little red schoolhouse" in the Talbot County driving tour. The last in the County, this building is thought to have been part of Wye Church's original parish house. The schoolroom lets the children know how it used to be when every classroom didn't have a computer.

"Wye" not float down the ol' mill stream and see old Wye Mill? This mill is definitely old. It looks old. In 1617 mill stones started grinding corn into meal and wheat seed into buckwheat flour, and still do.

The old mill's stream is divided down the middle between Queen Anne's and Talbot Counties. There were border disputes from time to time, but over the years these two counties have learned to share the mill.

This old mill was where Robert Morris, financier of the Revolutionary War, bought his flour. He paid ten thousand pounds' sterling to get a load sent to George Washington's troops at Valley Forge. The soldiers may not have had shoes, but they did have the staff of life baked from the finest flour in the colonies.

"Wye" not stop at Wye Church, built in 1721 on top of the earlier foundation of a structure erected in the late seventeenth century, and restored in 1949. A spectacular edifice, where the pulpit, prayer desk and lectern hang from the north wall, typical of colonial churches in the south. The box pews are enclosed by very high sides mostly because of cold winter drafts. The floor is laid with deep red bricks brought to this country as ballast in ships. The Royal Arms of England hangs on the wall. Wye Church is a chapel of ease for the parish and often the preacher was a layman who wasn't allowed to preach his sermon from the pulpit, even though he was ordained, only because he didn't have the proper vestry clothes. (In other words, he wasn't properly attired.)

Quakers and Puritans were, to say the least, at odds with one another, but both have contributed to Talbot County's formation. Both came in droves to settle in the County because of Lord Baltimore's Tolerance Act which granted freedom of worship to all. The Quakers governed themselves, taking care of the old and infirmed, and managed to get along with their neighbors, the Puritans.

Third Haven, the old Quaker's meetinghouse, was once on the edge of Easton. Now it is snuggled amongst private residences near a major highway and not easily found. If you are lucky enough to spot the wooden sign, you will drive between immense pines on a somewhat bumpy road, at the end of which is the meetinghouse. This place of worship is a small white frame structure, built in 1682, and lovingly cared for by the Quakers, whose

custom is to have meetings (church services are called meetings in the Quaker faith) there once a year.

The Quaker's Third Haven Meetinghouse was built in 1682, and is supposed to be the oldest frame building dedicated to religion in the United States. (And who would question?) William Penn once conducted a meeting under a big tree on the grounds and Lady Baltimore was believed to have attended, once. These gatherings drew, besides the devout, an unsavory lot who tippled to excess, among other undesirable activities, and made a circus out of what was meant to be solemn. The Quakers lost patience and finally had to prevail on the law to suppress such "goings-on" as were taking place.

These early meetings were held in the old unheated building with no soft cushions on the hard benches. Some members got so cold that they insisted wood stoves be installed and cushions provided for the seats. Well, many of the worshippers felt that cushions were too much of a creature comfort! A compromise was reached and half were removed. You are welcome to attend, but you might want to bring your stadium seat.

One of the most illustrious of the Puritans was Edward Lloyd, a man of varied abilities. He was a politician, an expert surveyor, a fur trader, a planter, a merchant, a tobacco buyer, an agent for immigrants and a superb negotiator who managed to keep peace between the Quakers and the Puritans.

Lloyd was granted five thousand acres in Talbot County as a gesture by the Puritan Board of Commission, of which he was a member, when they were ousted in favor of Lord Baltimore's appointed governor. He moved to Talbot County from Providence, Rhode Island, the first Puritan settlement in America, and built Wye House. A long succession of Lloyd men have become prominent in the County's affairs.

The mother of Edward Lloyd II and Richard Bennett III, Henrietta Maria Lloyd, was the wife of Philemon Lloyd I's son, and was one of the wealthiest and most influential social butterflies of her time. She married twice and bore her first husband, Richard Bennett, two sons and her second husband, Philemon Lloyd, ten children. She ran Wye House, after Lloyd expired in 1685, until her death in 1697.

"Madame," as she was always called, a title coveted in those times, gave one the same status as a lady-in-waiting did in England. Her remarkable assets, great beauty, charm, wealth, power and an independent personality bestowed on her the title, "great ancestor of the Eastern Shore." Her one son, Edward Lloyd II, became Governor of Maryland.

Interestingly, Henrietta was a Roman Catholic at a time when Papists were unpopular in Maryland. She was so strong-willed that her husband was forced to write into his will that his ten children were to be raised as Protestants.

In 1689 an "army," led by Richard Sweatnam, who kept the inn at the York Courthouse, stormed Wye House demanding that Madame Lloyd relinquish arms and armament stored in the house which could be used by the Catholics and Indians (yes, there were still Indians in Talbot County then) against the English. She held out and later sued Sweatnam and received a public apology. Her great wealth was reflected in her vast wardrobe and precious jewelry which dazzled Talbot's social circle, those who had begun to think of themselves as aristocrats, even though many started out as dirt farmers. Henrietta's credentials were impeccable. She was born in Spain, the daughter of James Neale, a man close to Cecilus Calvert, who represented Calvert at various courts in Europe. Her mother, Ann Gill Neale, was said to be Lady-in-waiting to Queen Henrietta Maria, the wife of Charles I. The Queen, it is believed, was Henrietta's godmother. She had a death's-head ring, now in the possession of the Talbot County Historical Society, given to her mother for her loyalty by the Queen after Charles I was beheaded. In the Lloyd graveyard at Wye House are ten generations of the family.

The inscription of her gravestone reads:

"She who now takes her rest within this tomb,
Had Rachells face and Leas fruitful womb,
Abigails wisdom, Lydeas faithful heart,

With Marthas care and Marys better part.
Who died the 21st day of May [Anno]
Dom. 1697 50 years --
months 23 days.
to whose memory Richard Bennett dedicates this tomb."

(Henrietta is spoken of because, in those days gone by, there are few females who gained such prominence as she and who would have made a splash in today's "enlightened" society.)

Easton is a posh town, much more cosmopolitan than most on the Shore. The first newspaper and the first bank on the Shore started in Easton. Her early names were "Talbot Town" and then "Talbot Courthouse" when the town was designated the sub-capital of Maryland. Today she is proud to be known as the "Colonial Capital of Maryland's Eastern Shore."

As you come into town, you are struck by the post office building whose architecture would not be out of place in Colonial Williamsburg. The historic buildings of Easton's past are interspersed with the present. The Courthouse, where the Talbot Resolves were made in May 1774, is the center of town. The elegant old structure is framed by the surrounding buildings which gives the feeling of a colonial capital. On the lawn there are picnic tables and large shade trees, a spot popular with the brown-baggers. The Market House, next to the courthouse, was the slave market where both tobacco and slaves were sold until after the Civil War. The "Frame Hotel," a century and a half old, is close by the Thomas-Perrin-Smith House, built in 1759. Smith was the publisher of the old Republican Star that, in 1855, became the Star-Democrat, one of the oldest daily papers in the country.

The Tavern of the Seven Stars was run by Josiah Coleman as late as 1744. His pub was a place of activity, a place you might compare to the general stores that came later, a place to share a brew and dawdle with friends. The tavern was where the "freemen" adjourned after so eloquently expressing their position on the Stamp Act. They toasted King George, still loyal to the Crown, they felt he was deceived by Parliament and held him blameless--for a time. The tavern is owned by the County's historical society.

The historical society, located in Easton, has a fine complex composed of several structures. A new auditorium, above the church next door, has been renovated and will be used for programs of local interest. Inside the entrance to the main building is a large room where constantly changing exhibits are displayed. The upper level has been restored as a typical home of the early eighteenth century.

Between the historical society's building and the Neall's home, there is an enclosed garden with white wrought-iron chairs and a table ready for afternoon tea. Behind the raised brick tea party area, which is blocked off from the street by a high red brick wall, is an herb and flower garden. Along one side are two small buildings authentic to the period. One was Mary Jenkins' home and is rented out from time to time. No word as to who Mary Jenkins might have been, but alas, probably no one knows. Joseph Neall's, a Quaker cabinetmaker, home dates from 1810 and has been furnished in representative period pieces. The doors in this old house are low (people were much shorter then) and wide (maybe they were fatter too), at least four feet. The trim takes your eye. Those sparkling big brass latches have keyholes large enough to see what's taking place on the other side. The rooms seem sparse, and they are. Only the necessities, no comfy couches, no wall-to-wall carpet, no overstuffed chairs. Life then was austere at best.

The hardwood floorboards are extra wide and have a patina that shines still. The fireplace is stand-up size and there is a grandfather's clock of great beauty, probably made by one of Neall's apprentices, an ever-changing group of men who came to learn under one of the finest cabinetmakers on the Shore. During Neall's eight years in Easton, he had eighteen apprentices.

The twelve chairs in the dining room are Chippendale style, as are most of the pieces. The bricks in the floors are laid in intriguing patterns differing in each room, something you see in other old houses, perhaps, since few had rugs, this was a way of decorating. All rooms have fireplaces to heat, but no indoor plumbing, and the kitchen was generally detached from the main house. It seems that the kitchen in this house was added along with the dining room. The floor in the new wing slants quite noticeably to the corner. The dishes are pewter and kept in a corner cabinet. Few had china, it was a luxury not available to a man who worked with his hands. Most of the utensils in the kitchen are copper and bright, as if the lady of the house had just polished them. There is a large spice rack, very important as food was often "ripe" when it came to the cook. There is a plaque displayed on an easel so we will all know how it was then. It says:

"Come Patty, my good little Mard. Let me have all the thing in ordering. Move quickly we must, so you can make the crust and mind to crimp the crust nicely the border." (Don't blame the writer for this use of the English language.)

The upstairs master bedroom is a large room, large because this is where the Neall's nine children spent their days. There is a crib in the ready, just in case, and a four poster bed. The Williamsburg green hangings on the bedposts and the exquisite hand-done French-knot spread, made by an aunt of Francis Scott Key and given to the society by a member, makes this room special. The chamber pot, generally kept under the bed, gives you an idea of how it was then. On the wall is an impressive silhouette of a grandmother of the period, the most respected member of all Quaker families.

To show off the craft of the artisan, there is a mock-up, in the backyard, of a typical woodworking shop with tools that school children can handle, and many do as they come in bunches to tour the museum of the past.

Across the street is a fine gift shop, so tastefully done with items for the kitchen in the kitchen, and in the dining room, things for the table, china and crystal that tempts one. The large front room is a book buyer's paradise with lots to choose from. If you are curious about where bathrooms were added to old homes, then ask where the ladies' room is. You will find only one facility, neatly tucked under the stairs with a door requiring you to duck down a bit. (Ingenious these folks.)

The old Avalon Theater, opened as a silent movie and vaudeville palace in 1921 with an elegant art deco style and marvelous marquee, has been restored and reopened as a theatre for the performing arts. The original candy machine is still there and you can get a miniature bar for a nickel, sometimes. A scale, where the top plate announces "Your Weight and Fortune and How Much Do You Weigh? One Cent. Guard Your Health," is not always accurate, but fun.

You cannot help but notice the elegant Tidewater Inn. The Federal style of architecture with the portico flying American flags makes an impression. The superb dining room, serving the finest Eastern Shore cuisine, and the common room, where the fire glows like the "publik" houses of colonial times, is a blend of the best of both periods.

When it was decided to have a wildfowl festival in Easton as a way of preserving the art form of the duck decoy carver, an idea was born that has become a bonanza for the town. As a result, over two million dollars has been donated to various conservation groups and the duck carvers are kept carving.

The festival has grown over the years to include: goose and duck calling contests (you haven't heard anything until you hear the call of the wild goose and the honk of the duck portrayed by humans!), wildfowl photography, an antique decoy auction, a federal duck stamp exhibit and a Chesapeake Bay Retriever (the state dog of Maryland) demonstration, with the working dogs performing under simulated field conditions.

You can be a part of all this which, naturally, includes eats and drinks and be merrys. It is a bit of a crowd, something like 5th Avenue in New York City during the Easter Parade. No way can you get your car into Easton, but there are designated parking areas and shuttle buses to get you back and forth. If you have an old festival book that's been on the shelf for some time, you might want to take it to the auction where it could reap a profit. Old duck decoys are at a premium, too, and if you've got one that you have been using as a doorstop, you might want to bring it along.

Do not miss the duck and goose calling contest, the most hilarious contest ever. Don't mean to poke fun...this is serious business if you are a honker or quacker imitator. Both the national and regional contests are held at this time. A favorite for the children, and all dog lovers, is the working dog show. You will be amazed at the skills these hunting dogs display. It's a ducky day to be in Easton cueing up for a look into the elegant Gold Room of the Tidewater Inn where the top twenty entries in the commemorative duck stamp competition show off their artistic talents.

The duck doings are in late October; but if you happen to be in Talbot County and it is August, you might go to a tournament which is a festival of the days when Richard the Lionhearted and knights of old jousted. The participants are not really knights, but seem so, dressed in the garb of those times with their ladies in the cone-shaped hats with the scarves hanging from the end and dresses cut scandalizingly low just like the ladies of yore wore. Sleek steeds race up and down while the riders try to hook a little ring on their pointed lances. No sport is more colorful than jousting. The horses are draped like those of the knights in the days of chivalry. The colors of the riders fly high and streamers decorate the judges' stand. A jolly good time -- for all. This tournament has been held in Talbot County since 1861 at the oldest Catholic Church on the Shore, St. Joseph's.

One of the busiest roads in colonial days ran from Oxford to White Marsh Church and on to Dover in Delaware. On the way to Oxford, on this road, is a hamlet, hardly even that, which for over two hundred years was called Hole-In-The-Wall, now Hambleton after a prominent Talbot family of whom Captain William Hambleton is the best remembered.

Hole-In-The-Wall is a name well chosen to describe the most infamous place existing then in this out of the way spot. A tavern in the town was a hangout for scummy sailors who smuggled. To hide the identity of both the

smuggler and his co-conspirator, the goods were pushed through the hole in the wall.

Another yarn about names is No Corner For The Devil. This is the name of the hexagonal structure, built in 1881, which served as a church for the Methodist, Reformed Lutheran, Swedenborgian and the Brethren, each having the use of the No Corner For The Devil building one Sunday in four. There is no chance of running into the devil because the six sides, with their wide angles, leave no corners for the devil to hide in.

Names of towns, like Trappe, can be intriguing. Possibly, but not for certain, the name comes from the order of French monks who had a monastery in the area or could have come from a tavern named the Partridge Trap, an extremely unpopular spot with the Methodists, who considered the tavern to be where the devil filled his quota for that place no one wants to go. Trappe was a crossroads town that by 1850 had reached a population of one hundred and ninety-eight folks, making Trappe the third largest town in Talbot County, at that time.

There were as many as eight general stores in the area. Barter was practiced then and the farmer's wife could trade her eggs for a new hair bow. There were three doctors, five shoemakers (no store-bought shoes then), seven carpenters (you built your own house with the help of the carpenters), two tailors (you had your clothes made too), a tanner (to make your leather jacket) and one hotel, also four churches. The streets were paved with (no, not gold) oyster shells and the board sidewalks lasted until after World War II. They had rules to keep things quiet around town, for example: a curfew horn sounded every night at 9:30 after which "quiet should be restored within the limits of the city." On Saturday night folks could stay out to 10 o'clock. Violators were fined 50 cents if white and, if not, were subject to ten lashes on the bare back. (Incredible, isn't it?) The speed limit was eight miles per hour and stayed that way well into the time of the automobile. All that is left of historical note is the Kemp House, dating from 1810, and the Dickerson House, built in the 1700s. (You **can** understand why this is almost all that is left, can't you?)

Along the road to Oxford you will pass long driveways disappearing into the woods. The lanes lead to the secluded homes of the rich and famous, whose estates face the Tred Avon River. Most have small, discrete signs with fanciful names and dates of their estates' beginnings ...unless the date is in the 1900s, then no date.

Tred Avon, nice sounding name, makes one think of ol' England and Shakespeare's home, Stratford-on-Avon. There is a feeling of Great Britain in this area. It is reflected in the many homes which are built of small square sections attached to the main house.

Pirates liked to hide out in the secluded peninsula on the way to Oxford and often laid over. Edward Teach, Blackbeard, Stede Bonnet and other disreputables would pose as Quakers, calling themselves "The Brethren." Some Spanish doubloons and pieces of eight showed up in the Talbot County school fund in 1750.

Marching, as if to God, a row of ancient cedars line the road into the Oxford Cemetery. Neatly trimmed and well kept, this burial ground spans the years. Along a cove of Town Creek are the old graves where several generations of Tilghmans are at rest. The still water of the cove reflects the green marsh grasses. Almost hidden by trees, across the mirrored surface, is the ancestral home of this family, Phimhimmon.

An obelisk stands in front of Tench Tilghman's grave and you learn that his body was moved to Oxford Cemetery from Baltimore in 1973. His wife, Anne Marie, lies beside him along with several generations of Tilghmans.

What a man Tench Tilghman was! A real patriot who served his country. He was a staunch supporter of independence even though his father was a loyalist. The story most often heard is that Tilghman carried the news of the victory at Yorktown to Annapolis riding horseback all the way. He was supposed to have stopped only for a fresh steed. Actually, he went by boat from Yorktown to Rock Hall in Kent County and **then** on horseback to Annapolis. His epitaph is a tribute from George

Washington who said, "He had as fair a reputation ever belonged to a human character," quite a compliment from the father of our country.

Oxford, once briefly known as Williamstadt, has ties to the family of the third Lord Baltimore, Charles. It seems that Colonel Vincent Lowe, brother of Lady Baltimore, was one of the commissioners named to lay out the town. His wife, Elizabeth Foster, gave the land for the town's site. Colonel Lowe's sister, Jane Lowe Sewell, was married to Charles Calvert in 1666. He was Royal Governor of Maryland before becoming the third Lord Baltimore.

Can you believe how different Oxford would be if the town had been named the county seat? It would now have the colonial courthouse, the streets would have quadrupled, the marina would be larger and there probably wouldn't be a ferry to Bellevue, a bridge would be more likely, and all that is part of downtown Easton would be in Oxford. One wonders, with the town surrounded by water, where all of Easton would be. That problem was solved when Easton became the county seat.

Robert Morris was a man in the right place at the right time, 1738. He represented one of the great trading companies in Liverpool, England, and came to do business in Oxford. He also dabbled in a few ventures on his own, but shipping tobacco to England, where there was a great demand for Maryland's tobacco, made him a wealthy man. His home was along the water on the Strand. (The street bordering the river is called the Strand, a word the dictionary defines as "the land bordering a body of water.") While sitting in an open boat receiving the tribute due him, a twenty-one gun salute (well maybe not twenty-one, but a salute), wadding from one of the ship's guns hit him in the arm. Infection from this wound caused his death six days later. It is he who is buried in White Marsh Cemetery, next to the ruins of White Marsh Church.

His fortune came to his son, Robert Morris, Jr., known as the financier of the American Revolution, whom he had brought over from England when junior was only thirteen. (Nothing is mentioned of the boy's mother.) Young Robert Morris left Talbot County to live in

Philadelphia, where he became friendly with George Washington. He gave his personal fortune to finance the American Revolution and is remembered for this patriotic act.

If you were there when Oxford was a royal port, you would be dressed a bit differently. If you were a lawyer, you wore a white powdered wig when you went to court, otherwise, you had a pigtail, knee britches and silk stockings, all topped by fancy brocaded vests, and a waistcoat. Your lady had her hair piled high on her head, lace trimmed the cuffs of her floor-length dress, just like the front of your shirt, and her neckline was cut to show a cleavage that would shock today's female. You would be in Oxford to attend the races, and important social, as well as sporting, events. Gambling, tippling and dancing were the order of the day in Oxford's golden years. You would lead an idle life and swagger and boast a lot. No doubt you would have your own bird and enter him in cockfights. The highborn ladies of that time were "often haughty, overbearing and vindictive in spirit," wrote Jeremiah Banning, the favorite son of Oxford, in a narrative journal of his life compiled five years before his death in 1798.

Jeremiah Banning was appointed customs officer by George Washington, who knew him during the Revolution. In his journal, Jeremiah, described Oxford as a thriving port with sailing ships coming and going constantly. Tall-masted schooners, with yards and yards of canvas, sailed up the Choptank River into the Tred Avon. It was common to see as many as eight oceangoing vessels in one day unloading their cargos. Amongst these large sailing ships were the beautiful bateaux and the fast-moving log canoes all laden with goods from across the Atlantic.

The adorable replica of the original customs house sits along the Strand, but in Jeremiah's day it was on Plaindealing Creek. It is a small, square structure with an oversized window looking out on the water and a fireplace to warm one on cold winter days.

Look out the window, you can almost see the tall-masted ships maneuvering in and out of the port. The docks were piled high with hogsheads of tobacco, yards of fine linen, crates of English bone china, boxes of

silverware and fancy goods for milady, all waiting to be loaded on horse-drawn wagons for delivery to Easton.

As romantic as it seems, everyone was not in a position to import goods. The holds of these fine sailing ships were crammed with men, women and their children who came to America to work off their obligation as indentured slaves. Some ships held as many as a hundred prisoners packed body to body. These "slaves," mostly white, were not a pretty sight when they arrived and the captains spent a time dolling them up for "market." The men were clean shaven and the women dressed in their best. The auction was a social get-together with kegs of rum for buyers to enjoy while they inspected the prisoners for imperfections. Families were torn apart and carted off to work the tobacco plantations.

Captain Banning was much stricken by these slave auctions, and if he had been around during the Civil War, he would certainly have been an abolitionist. He had slaves, however, he treated them more like servants than slaves. In his will he listed specific items to go to each and every one.

The port of Oxford's golden years were short-lived, and after the Revolutionary War the harbor was deserted. British ships no longer called at Oxford. English firms were out of business, the warehouses were empty and tobacco was slipping as a crop. The clipper ship, the most beautiful of all the sailing vessels, who once were built in Oxford and St. Michaels, were being built in Baltimore.

Jeremiah Banning described Oxford after the Revolution in these words, "The poor, drooping, and forsaken Oxford, bereft of almost every comfort in life, hath nothing remaining to console itself but its salubrious situation and fine navigation which may anticipate better times. Oxford, where streets and strands were once covered with busy, noisy crowds, ushering in commerce from almost every quarter of the Globe, and whose rich, blooming lots echoed with fair growing kind, alas, now is shaded by wheat, corn and tobacco. The once well-worn streets are now grown up with grass, save a few tracks made by sheep and swine;

and the strands have more the appearance of an uninhabited island than where human feet have ever trod."

Jeremiah Banning was a captain at age twenty-two and voted as a delegate for ratification of the Constitution of the United States of America. To the people of Oxford, he best represents the way of life in the late 1700s.

A lot of slaves, from Talbot County, were sold south before the Civil War because cash was offered, a commodity rare in the County in the 1820s. A plan to send the blacks back to Africa was supported, even welcomed. The gift of a ship, the <u>Maryland Caroline Steven</u>, to transport the blacks back to Liberia, was a bequest in the will of John Stevens. So far as is known, none ever migrated. The slaves were many times removed from their African ancestors and didn't want to leave their Eastern Shore homes for a strange land where they no longer spoke the language.

Frederick Douglass, the renowned orator and writer, who was not only firmly against slavery but also believed in women's right to vote, was born the son of a slave, at Tuckahoe Creek in Talbot County. When he was twenty, in 1838, he escaped north and changed his name from Frederick Bailey to Frederick Douglass. He was as much a symbol in his time as Martin Luther King, Jr., was in the twentieth century.

Douglass was better known in Europe than Abraham Lincoln and was received by Queen Victoria. He advised Lincoln during the Civil War, was United States Marshall and Recorder of Deeds for the District of Columbia. If King and Douglass had known each other, they would have been compatriots.

The age of innocence gripped the Eastern Shore with the arrival of the steamboats and the railroads. The world again opened to Oxford. In the years to follow, Oxford's population rose from two hundred and seventy-seven souls to seven hundred and fifty. Resort hotels went up along the Strand. The Robert Morris Inn was enlarged and became a popular vacation spot called

Riverview House.   Next door to the old inn, was a bowling alley and, in the rear, a livery stable.

The inn has a checkered history. After the high time for Oxford, the Robert Morris Inn regained its original name and was, in 1921, used as quarters for blind veterans from World War I and later as a general store with a cafe and gas pump out front. A fire destroyed almost all of the original building and only a small portion dates to the time of Robert Morris. Of the original, besides the beautiful staircase, there is the Georgian white pine flooring in the upstairs hall, and four of the guest rooms have handmade paneling and fireplaces of bricks made in Britain and used as ballast in sailing ships. The impressive murals in the dining room were from wallpaper samples used by manufacturers' salesmen one hundred and forty years ago and printed on screw-type presses using sixteen hundred woodcut blocks carved from orangewood.

Mrs. John F. Kennedy found the original wallpaper, of the design in a western Maryland home, and had it removed and put on the walls of the White House Reception Room. The Riverview Room has two hundred and sixty year old wall panels, but the tavern's slate floor, which came from Vermont, and over the fireplace the Morris coat of arms, a magnificent oak wood, deep relief by John White, and the hand-carved log canoe with sails full makes the taproom the most interesting. Of this inn James A. Michener, while writing Chesapeake, said that he rated the crab cakes the highest rating of any restaurant on the Shore. "I go to the Robert Morris Inn frequently for their good crab cakes...raise a glass of beer in memory of an old-timer who enjoyed the place very much." (This author was knocked dead by the size of the succulent oyster sandwich, a house specialty.)

Outside the inn the flag of the original thirteen states flies. You see a lot of American flags flying in Oxford. Tells you something, doesn't it? The strip of sand along the river in front of the inn is still there, but the boarding houses that lined the Strand are not.

During this period, Town Park was spruced up. Trees were planted and the only school in town was moved to the north end of the two-acre park. Plans for a new church on Kerr's Island, connected by a causeway, never materialized. Two very long wharves, one at City Dock and one at the south end of town, linked with the railroad which arrived in 1871. Two smaller docks on Town Point were busy with steamboats coming and going. The Tred Avon Yacht Club is located there today. Oyster shucking, packing and canning plants started up and shipbuilding began again. The best of the best, William P. Benson and Nathaniel Leonard, master boat builders, moved in at a site on Town Creek and began building bugeyes, a working boat that preceded the skipjack and was the watermen's favorite at that time. If you ask why they were called bugeyes, you will get a variety of responses, but the consensus of opinion is that the two round spots of each side of the bow looked like a bug's eye.

Oxford's homes, the fences surrounding them, and the red brick sidewalks leading past them, are the most unique on the Shore, in all of Maryland, perhaps in all of America. If you take time, you will notice that the bricks in the sidewalk are different patterns, as are the fences in front, a sort of staking out one's territory by the watermen who broke with tradition and faced their homes away from the water.

The walkways are zigzag patterns of four squares or two squares, but none the same. The only similarity found is in the shape of the letter "B" stamped randomly on some of the bricks, which stood for the Bergman brickyard on the edge of town.

The wrought-iron fences are all iron, but different in pattern and shapes of the dofunnys, thingumadoodles and domajiggers as are the large Victorian homes. This individuality in trim around doors, windows and roofs is called, in Oxford, "Carpenter's Gothic"...a style by which each craftsman left their mark in doodads, thingumabobs, dohickeys and thingumajigs. Lots of time can be spent by trying to tell the thingumadoods from the dohickeys.

The streets' names remain the same as in the first plat, but you might be confused if you looked at the plan because there is no road coming into town, making the map appear upside down. There wouldn't have been any road on the plan because everyone came by boat then.

For a time, the railroad and the steamboat combined to put the Bay side of the Eastern Shore on the map. Wharfs appeared and little waysides burst into bustling resort towns. The automobile did in Oxford as it did in most places along the shoreline that relied on transportation by rail or water. It is hard to believe that Oxford's boat yard was so large, with docks and buildings spread all over the point. It is hard to imagine that there was a seafood packing plant, with several sheds, and an engine manufacturing company, at the end of Pier Street, all of which have left no indication of their ever having been in Oxford.

As you drive into town along Morris Street, you notice a rather large community center for such a small town. You catch a glimpse of Town Creek and the marina with big-buck boats who share their space with fishing skiffs. The homes at the edge of town are modest, with most having screen porches. You soon come upon the "shopping center" called the Mews, appropriately English. (The dictionary defines the word mews as coming from "the royal stable in England so called because built where the king's hawks were mewed or confined"), which explains the black iron hitching posts out front with horses' heads and brass rings to tie up your steed. It is an old building, not historic, but old with white posts holding up the sagging roof that extends over the sidewalk. A lot of bikes lean against the white wood siding waiting for riders, a good way to see Oxford and get a bit of exercise. You can take the bikes on the Oxford-Bellevue Ferry and ride along the back roads past farm after farm on the way to St. Michaels.

A business of note in the Oxford Mews is the bike "boatique" (clever). You can buy or rent a bike or have yours repaired, or purchase bike and yacht accessories, or prime beef, chops, spices, sweets, condiments and jams, which only partly describes the vast selection of possible purchases. The Bike Boatique is tiny, with shelves that reach above your head and are packed so tight together you can't get a finger hold on the jar of olives and have to tip it off. You push past the stacks of miniatures merchandise (to accommodate the boating crowd, one suspects) packed on the shelf in the center aisle. Stepping carefully, you get to the back where everything for use on your bike or yacht (never call yachts, boats) is available. Off to the right is an oversized closet-like room with a fine collection of books, largely on Maryland and sailing. Actually if you are in Oxford, you came there to sail or to sightsee, so the books are appropriate. The walking tour guide of Oxford is for sale and is worth a buck. If you plan to do a lot of shopping, remember that this is not a mall, but a mews. Do not expect to find the Mews open on Wednesdays, Sundays, or in the evenings.

Next to the unique boatique is an art and artifact shop which has some fine watercolor pictures in the window, and beside the shopping complex is a Hershey's ice cream sign on a small market where you get a sandwich or buy a ticket to the Maryland Lottery, yes the lottery is popular even in Oxford. An emporium advertises antique furniture and that composes the whole of the Mews.

On Market Street is the Oxford Museum where the lady in charge will tell you the first name of the Tred Avon River was Third Haven, then Tred Haven, then Trade Haven, and that no one knows why it is now called Tred Avon. She will also tell you that the flavor of English culture still flowers among the oldest families. The museum shows what it was like in Oxford during the eighteenth century. There is a collection of memorabilia, simple things, that helps you picture the past. Upstairs, a room is turned into a ship's smith's shop with the "smithy" working on a piece of iron. The smithy was as important as any ship's captain. Ships needed to be in shipshape and the smithies kept them that way.

Besides the museum and the Oxford Mews, the only thing left in town to do is to take the walking tour and then sit on one of the park benches and contemplate the water. Exactly what none of the fishermen, who first built Oxford's homes, wanted to do. You will notice that all the homes on Morris Street face the street rather than the water. The reason being that after a hard day on the river, the fishermen did not want to look at any more water.

On the walking tour you will see Mary Stewart's home on Morris Street, which was both a home and the post office. She was appointed to succeed her father in 1877 and was postmistress for sixty-three years, the longest tenured head of a post office in United States' history. The most magnificent magnolia you ever saw is across the street and must be every bit of forty feet tall.

Some of the oldest homes in Oxford have interesting histories. One was a bakery and the baker, who had a pushcart, sold tasty tidbits from his cart to folks along the street. The house where Captain Richard Barnaby lived has a stone in the cellar with the date 1770 carved on it, and then there is the one with a vault, where a furrier used to keep skins he trapped at the proper temperature. The most popular attraction in Oxford is the Grapevine House, and everyone wants to see this vine, which most think of as almost totally covering the house. The vine, a veracious grape, was brought to America in 1785 from the Isle of Guernsey and survived the crossing by having its roots planted inside potatoes. The vine continues to spew forth grapes today, but trimmed to an arbor, it is not as obvious as expected.

An ambitious project, the Oxford Military and Naval Academy, begun by Colonel Tench Tilghman in 1847 with the intention of creating a second West Point, went out of business in a short time due to poor management. The Bratt family bought the lovely Academia House and moved it to Morris Street.

Oxford can claim as her citizens besides Robert Morris, Sr., Colonel Tench Tilghman and Jeremiah Banning, Reverend Thomas Bacon, Anglican clergyman, who wrote the first compilation of the Laws of Maryland, and Matthew Tilghman, known as the "patriarch of Maryland" and "father of statehood."

The few descendants of the old families remaining in Oxford are slowly adjusting to the inevitable changes occurring in town. The Tred Avon Yacht Club's members

are mostly the descendants of the old families, but encroachments are being made. Along the water is a new condo complex and new faces can be seen on Morris Street. Town Park is still a quiet spot to rest and watch the sunset. Oxford can be described by the well-worn phrase as a place where the sidewalks are rolled up by 5 o'clock. It may not remain so, but change comes slowly to the Shore and Oxford will have to leave the past or accept death along with the other ghost towns of Talbot County. What the next century will bring, no one knows.

At the ferry dock is a historical marker that tells you the Oxford Ferry has plied the river since 1836 when the "Talbot County Court pitched upon Mr. Richard Royston to keep a ferry, to be run for horses and men." The ferry has undergone a number of changes. The sail, which powered her, was replaced by a large sweep oar, then by steam, in the form of a push tug, and, eventually, a diesel-powered engine, introduced in 1938 by Captain Bell Benson, who ran the ferry for forty years. The ferry is the oldest of its type (runs free, without cable) in continuous use in the United States, according to the historic marker.

The Oxford-Bellevue Ferry is not at all like the Lewes-Cape May Ferry, who runs across Delaware Bay to New Jersey and is the largest on the Shore. She is a tiny affair holding only nine cars, an upgrade from the previous one that held only three and was really a scow, with a sail. The ferry goes back and forth continually, but at different times depending on the season, no ferry a'tall from December 25 through February. You might very well be the only passenger.

On the other side the first thing you see is a lovely park with picnic tables and shady trees, a good spot to eat the sandwich you bought in Oxford. You are at Bellevue where once the Valliant Packing Company had several plants right where the ferry docks. They advertised, "where quality reigns" and did a rousing business. There is nothing left of this once busy town conceived by Oswald Tilghman, and named after his wife, Belle. He envisioned a resort, like Ocean City, but it didn't materialize and there is nothing of note now. (One wonders how Mr. Tilghman could have thought that

a resort like Ocean City could have possibly developed in such an isolated place as this.)

Route 329 is part of the state of Maryland's scenic highway system and is a pleasant ride past fertile farms populated by friendly folks. This area is thought of as "The Goose Capital of the World" and you can wile away a day listening to the songs of the birds. In fall and winter the honking of the geese will help you honk away your day on the one hundred and thirty-five peaceful acres, which composes the Pasadena Inn's land.

The Pasadena Inn opened in Royal Oak along with more than a half dozen boarding houses. During the good times, Royal Oak had two churches, five general stores, five blacksmiths, a barbershop and a business that served two functions--a funeral parlor and a carriage salesroom. A rumor went around that Royal Oak was the "healthiest place in America," a statement brought about by an advertisement in the St. Michaels Comet, for a piece of property for sale in Royal Oak. In an attempt to say something special, the editor went a bit overboard and printed, "according to unpublished statistics the health center of the United States is a circle with Royal Oak at the center of the four mile radius." A complete distortion, but the piece was picked up by the big city papers all over the United States.

The Pasadena Inn was opened in 1901 by Fred Harper, who called it Pasadena after the city in California where his family had moved. He advertised in the Washington and Baltimore papers, "summer boarders five dollars a week--children half rate." (Can you imagine!) The Harpers ran the inn for more than fifty years. Perhaps the reason it was so successful was that Gary Cooper slept there when he was filming a picture at the Inn at Perry Cabin called "The First Kiss," with Faye Raye, and everyone wanted to bed down in that very room. The Harpers made folks happy when they gave those who asked for **that** room, any room available and let them believe that it was **the** very room. (When you make a reservation, if you want to stay in **that** room, ask for number 35.)

During the War of 1812, when an attack on St. Michaels was expected, lanterns were hung in the trees in the hope of fooling the British into overshooting the town; it worked. However, one of the balls overshot St. Michaels and landed in a large oak tree in Royal Oak. The town is supposed to be named after this event, but don't be too sure. Some say it was named after a military company called Heart of Oak who fought in the Revolutionary War. (Sounds right.)

Past Royal Oak is St. Michaels, the town that fooled the British in the War of 1812. The harbor of the Miles River was an important shipbuilding center, a place where shipyards, and there were several, turned out sleek-hulled vessels, ones that would be known one day as the Baltimore clippers.

The most famous of shipbuilders, Thomas Kemp, built the clipper ship, the Chausseur, the most beautiful vessel that ever floated and, with her raked lines and top-heavy sails, was one of the fastest ships ever built. In three notable encounters, as a privateer, she captured British merchant ships, outraced the entire British Navy and whipped the armed schooner, St. Lawrence, in a fierce battle off Cuba. Her captain, Thomas Boyle, sailed boldly up the coast of England and declared a one-ship blockade of the entire British Isles. The Chausseur was the prototype for the first Pride of Baltimore.

The population then were the direct descendants of the Irish and Scotch immigrants who came to the New World as indentured slaves or convicts. These rough and ready laborers lived, what would be described today as, below the poverty line. Payday was the day these illiterate, totally undisciplined, workers cut loose with a vengeance. It was a rough and tumble time for St. Michaels until the Methodists moved in and put a stop to this disruptive behavior.

Sharp's Island, long since taken by Eastern Bay, was threatened by British warships. Admiral Warren captured the island and seized the livestock, for which he paid the owner, Jacob Gibson, cash. Jacob, a notorious prankster, was a tough type who liked a good brawl. A man who kept his name before the public by writing letters to the editor, pieces of a vicious nature, generally damning politicians, that the paper printed to increase circulation. Gibson hated the Federalists, loved the Jeffersonians, the French Revolution and a good knockdown, draw out fight with his fists. He kept in shape by doing his own farm work and was a formidable opponent. His tendency to practical jokes got him in more trouble than his pugnacious nature did.

Panic gripped the residents of St. Michaels when the word spread that an attack by British man-of-wars was imminent. As a joke, Gibson took his barge and floated up Broad Creek flying a banner that very much resembled the Union Jack. His servant beat a martial drum roll on an empty barrel as the barge headed straight for the dock.

Understandably, the residents of St. Michaels were frightened out of their wits (sorry trite, but right) by what they perceived to be an enemy ship. Remembrances of Admiral Cockburn's behavior at Hampton Roads, in Virginia, when he allowed his men to rape, plunder and burn the city, were fresh in their minds. The pride of St. Michaels, the Independent Light Dragoon and the Patriot Blues, military units, were called into action. The townsfolk went wild and everyone hid where they could. When it was discovered that this was another of Jacob's hoaxes, they were infuriated. He was summarily shunned by the best families. Ashamed of what he had done and in an attempt to redeem himself, he made a public apology, which did not bring him the desired absolution. In a final attempt to redeem himself, he presented the town with two cannons used during the British attacks.

In spite of Jacob Gibson's shortcomings, he was a perfect example of the spirit of democracy that permeated the country after the Revolution. He was described as "a stout-hearted, large-boned, strong-armed...friend of the poor, enemy of the rich and lofty...lifelong foe of autocratic pretensions and lover of democracy."

Word got out that the British, who had already landed two thousand troops on Kent Island, were expected to attack St. Michaels at any moment. Parrot Point was manned day and night by the militia who had taken an oath to fight to the death in defense of St. Michaels. When the first craft of the enemy flotilla nosed too close, these unseasoned young men fled like folks in a rainstorm.

One hero of the militia, John Stevens, remained behind. There was no ammunition, so Stevens loaded the cannon with bits of china, broken glass, spikes, nails and whatever he could find. Nineteen of the British troops were killed and only then did he run for cover. When the cannon balls ran out, the British, whose casualties were high, retreated to Kent Island to regroup and return another day, which they did.

It was a rainy night with no moon to light the town when, what is referred to as, the second battle of St. Michaels took place. The clever residents got the idea to put lit lanterns in the treetops in hopes of fooling the enemy into overshooting the town; it worked and the British were properly fooled. This perfectly marvelous tale has been embellished, as is the right of the descendants of those who did their part for freedom.

The small town of St. Michaels, estimated population of just over thirteen hundred (the census takers haven't counted them yet), has another story almost as good as the "town that fooled the British" and almost as exciting, but not as dangerous. When it was learned that the movie, "The First Kiss," was to be filmed in St. Michaels at the Inn at Perry Cabin, folks went wild. Most managed to get themselves signed up as extras and all the watermen and the entire fleet of skipjacks and bugeyes were hired for a princely sum.

This movie, considered to be the lousiest of the lousy, was a yarn about watermen which starred Gary Cooper, who no one ever heard of, and Faye Raye. Fay Raye found fame in a later movie as the occupant of the body that was waved from the top of the Empire State Building in the clutches of the hairy hand of King Kong. Absolutely miles of film was shot and the locals appeared in almost every reel.

The courtroom scene, the high-water mark of the movie, where "Coop" was charged with piracy, yes piracy, an illegal act that was supposed to have enabled him to send his three brothers to college. Over two hundred Talbotians appeared as judge, jury, witnesses and spectators. It was great fun and everyone waited with great expectations for the opening, which was held in Easton. Meanwhile back in Hollywood, the entire movie was being shot over using cardboard sets and professional actors. (This begins to sound like one of Gibson's tricks.) Needless to say, everyone in Talbot County, and particularly in St. Michaels, were disgruntled, except perhaps the Harper family who were packing 'em in at the Pasadena Inn.

The Inn at Perry Cabin, which seems to be a favorite of Hollywood for movies, was recently the site of the filming of a movie called "Clara's Heart," starring Whoopi Goldberg. The Inn, besides being a place popular with movie makers, is named after Commodore Hazard Perry. It seems that Captain William Hambleton had eleven children, one of whom, Samuel, joined the fledgling American Navy in 1806 as purser. He became a close friend of Oliver Perry and fought with the commander at the Battle of Lake Erie, where Perry's forces captured six enemy vessels. Hambleton thought so much of Perry that he named his estate near St. Michaels, "Perry Cabin." As fate will have it, Samuel's younger brother, who also joined the navy, was present at the death of Commodore Perry in 1819.

St. Michaels, little more than a grouping of small wooden homes surrounding the parish church back in 1805, has been touched by the "good witch of the north" who waved her wand and sprinkled glitter all over the buildings turning them into a rainbow of colors. This fairyland has more than you can imagine, and a good way to see it is by horse-drawn Brougham carriage, whose costumed driver will take you through the historic district and tell you lots about the town that fooled the British. (Getting tired of that phrase?) The driver will point out numerous trinket and knickknack shops, including a store where you can buy books on everything and everyone to do with the state of Maryland.

If you come into St. Michaels on a summer afternoon when the wind is up and the day is bright and the sun is shining, and you plan to tie up at the marina, forget it. Unless you arrive under the cover of darkness an hour or two before dawn, you will have to drop anchor and take the water taxi. Nothing wrong with that, actually it is easier than trying to find a slip to slip in.

It is all there, the early eighteenth century jammed in with the twentieth. The cannons Jacob Gibson tried to buy back his good name with are in St. Mary's Square, well not the originals but good replicas. St. Mary's Square is the center of activities in the town. The museum is in the middle of this large square of green grass and shade trees planted by James Braddock, who was sent from England to promote trade in St. Michaels.

The museum is in a building built in the 1700s and moved to the square from Maritime Museum Road. It is a house museum filled with things in use long ago and in the rear is a historic structure, once called "Teetotal," which was restored to its 1860s era and contains the community's memorabilia.

On the corner is the Cannonball House. This is another "town that fooled the British" story that has been embellished on equally as much as the Kitty Knight tall tale from the Revolutionary War. It seems that when all these cannonballs were flying overhead, one made a direct hit shaking this house dreadfully. The ball fell into the chimney, bounced down the steps and rolled out the front door. The only damage was to the finger of the lady of the house who was trying to keep her wits by quilting and pricked her finger with a needle. If you've heard that there is a big hole in the wall where the cannonball crashed through, don't believe it.

If you are wandering around and don't see one of the carriages, you might ride a bike. But if you do, you will have to ride in the street, because if you try the sidewalk, you will be walking beside your bike rather than riding on it. If you do ride a bike, you can peddle down streets with names like Muskrat Park and

Hell's Crossing, the old names for what is now Locust and Carpenter Streets.

Bike on down to the edge of town and park your bike at the Maritime Museum on Navy Point. The idea of a museum, to preserve the sailing heritage of the Eastern Shore, came from Bob Smith, a writer for the Star-Democrat, who kept nagging and nagging about the skipjacks and the bugeyes and the usual log canoes who were slipping away like the tide and would soon disappear with nothing left for the later generations to see how it used to be. His dream was realized in 1963 when, with the help of the Talbot County Historical Society, a strip of land down the middle of Navy Point was purchased and three old houses moved to the site. Mr. Smith was one of the early hired help whose title was "assistant curator."

As hired help he was always on call, so to speak, and many a cold night he was summoned from his warm bed to turn off the burglar alarm system which sounded whenever there was a thunder and lightning storm. Then there was the night the lightship's bell sounded a gong twice and Old Barney began backing out on her own heading somewhere. Mr. Smith's experiences could fill a book, he tells you.

The site of the Chesapeake Maritime Museum was once a tomato packing plant associated with Perry Cabin Farms. All of the buildings were moved from other places.

Outside the museum's entrance is the gift shop and book store. An iron Chesapeake Bay Retriever waits on the front porch for the children to straddle, keeps the younglings busy while you poke around among the fine collection of maritime books, histories, books with gorgeous photos and cookbooks that tell you how to make a fine Maryland crab cake. Then there are those adorable tiny models of fishing shanties on cork bases with crab pots on the pier and a fisherman mending his nets or lighthouses with gulls overhead and lots of tee shirts, mugs, hats and other items too numerous to mention. St. Michaels is emblazoned on almost everything. Some never get past the gift shop into the

museum, and that is too bad because the collection is one of the finest of the Bay museums in Maryland.

You purchase a ticket at the pilot house, all that is left of the Annapolis buy boat. (Buy boats bought the fisherman's catch.) Instead of corn, the eighteenth century corncrib holds all types of fishing crafts used by watermen, kinds you've heard of but never seen. A sink box, that raft with the square box in the middle for the watermen to sit in, and duck decoys covering the wood boards holding the raft together, was legal when a man gunned for the dinner table...no duck, no dinner. But when duck became a table delicacy, during the Gay Nineties, some who once hunted for the evening meal now gunned for the gentry and were called "Ploggers." Ploggers averaged ten thousand ducks a year, nearly wiping out the duck population. The sort of gunning boats used by the Ploggers, the sink box, the icebox and the bushwhacker on show, are outlawed today.

The museum took off in 1966 when the Hooper Straight Lighthouse was barged sixty miles north and set on legs giving it the appearance of a daddy-longlegs. This cottage-type light first flashed a beacon in 1876 to guide ships from the mouth of the Patuxent River into the Bay. Inside this hexagon house, the designer managed to include a kitchen (a nice one), two bedrooms and a parlor with a picture window view of the Miles River. If you could read the keeper's log, you would know that it was a lonely existence, being a light keeper, particularly since your wife and family were only allowed to visit two weeks of the year.

It was a long trip by boat to the general store, but then you didn't have to cut the grass. Men who kept the light had their own special reward, they knew all the ships in site of the beacon depended on the shining lamp to light their way. For most, this was enough. The light now flashes CBMM (Chesapeake Bay Maritime Museum) every fifteen seconds to let sailors know the museum's light is what they see.

Beside the lighthouse is the Point Lookout Bell Tower, a one thousand pound bell which rang for more than one hundred years to warn ships off the shallows where the Potomac River meets the Bay.

Tolchester, a resort of some note along the Bay in Kent County, has nothing left but a few concrete steps where some fading paint tells you this is the way to the bathhouse. The bandstand, where families gathered to listen to songs like "Daisy, Daisy, Give Me Your Answer True, For I Am Half Crazy All For The Love Of You" and "Come With Me On My Flying Machine", is now at the museum. Folks come to hear the old songs on nice summer evenings, just as they once did at Tolchester.

The imposing Chesapeake Bay Building has twenty-four-foot ceilings allowing a fishing skiff, in full sail, to wait for the tide that never comes. In this place you learn about the Chesapeake of the past with numerous models, first-class illustrations, paintings and artifacts that trace the life on the Bay from prehistoric time, the time of the Indians, the colonial era, the War of 1812 and the Civil War, to the present. One special display is the wheel from President Lincoln's River Queen, his headquarters from March 23, 1865, until his assassination.

The aquarium is a constantly changing collection of the aquatic life in the Bay and is dependent on the fishing skills of the museum staff to replace what fish has been eaten by its companion.

Besides fishing skills, boat builders' skills are honed daily as they keep in shape the ever increasing collection of Bay boats including, a bugeye, a log canoe, an oyster buy boat and a Virginia crabber. The skipjack Rosie Parks sunk below the surface one day and is replaced by the E. C. Collier.

Hunters and collectors come from all over the world to see the extensive array of duck decoys in the Wildfowl Building. These "working" decoys have been coupled, in the display, with the wave of the future in the duck decoy world, the art form of duck decoy, the kind you don't put in the water. The gun collection is extensive and superb including modern firearms as well as those used by Ploggers. The "Twombley", a gun which rose to fame in Michener's Chesapeake, and an eight-barrel swivel gun are there along with many others.

Plans for the future include a propulsion building, a reproduction of the steamboat terminal in Claiborne and a wharf where real people do what they used to do when St. Michaels was a fishing village. In the proposed propulsion display you will see steam engine models, the internal combustion engine, dredges, pumps, generators and hydraulic engines. An outstanding collection of photos picturing steamboats who plied back and forth from Baltimore to the Eastern Shore in the early 1900s will fill a wall, and a video will take you on a steamer "trip" down the Bay in the 1930s.

Don't miss the docks where the floating fleet is moored. This pier of yesteryear makes you realize how fast things come and go. You cannot help but feel a wrench in your stomach as you look at these lovely ladies of the sea who will never again feel the wind in their sails.

You can drift along the Miles River on a tour boat and learn a bit about ecological facts while you enjoy a ninety-minute cruise. The skipper points out the sights along the river, which is not a true river but an estuary, therefore, there is no head but there is a mouth, the winding river empties into Eastern Bay. Pointed out are where all the steamboat landings used to be, and numerous Ospreys' nests, where if it is spring, you will see both mama and papa waiting for the little one. Osprey mate for life and generally return to the same spot to breed again. Those on the river are atop the channel markers and easy to see. The eels that no one eats, except the Europeans, are harvested in the beds where crabs are still sleeping deep below. These slimy things are actually catching on, but only for the few who want to cook eels for themselves.

You will see sailing boats of all kinds, if it is the weekend when you are there--if not, mostly working boats. The captain tells you that the Miles River was once called the St. Michaels. The Quakers and the Puritans got rid of the "saint" immediately and the name Michaels was slowly corrupted to Miles. (Maybe, but couldn't the Puritans have called it Miles, after Miles Standish? No one can be sure.)

If you've been to St. Michaels and the maritime museum and on the tour boat, drive right on through and head for Tilghman Island, but do not miss Claiborne. What glorious plans were made for Claiborne and for a while it appeared the dreams might come true. Plans were for two hundred lots facing Eastern Bay on eight different main streets and when things really got rolling, the name Claiborne would be changed to Bay City. The owner of the sawmill, Joseph T. Tunis, decided to advertise, since he was also a real estate person and had a vested interest in seeing this planned town come to fruition. "Young men, don't go West, but to Claiborne." Everyone hoped they would come, but they didn't. One of the reasons was the planned town was poorly planned and was placed, in the plans, across the creek from where the steamboat landing was.

It was a busy time for the steamboats, the railroad and the car ferry who left Claiborne for Annapolis on a regular basis. The railroad was nicknamed the "Cinder and Ashes Line" for obvious reasons if you know anything a'tall about old trains. This smoky railroad stopped at St. Michaels, Easton, Salisbury and Berlin, and whistle stops along the route. There was even a lay over hotel for employees, and along the water, a number of rooming houses. Maple Hill, one of the better known, managed to stay open until 1967. A fine looking home, "Wade's Point," was built by Thomas Wade, the well-known shipbuilder from Fell Point in Baltimore. It was so popular a spot for visitors that his wife finally had to charge rates for her rooms, no one minded though. It was the kind of summer place that the song of the same name makes you think of, and still is. Wade's Point is the spot where the British first set foot on American soil in the War of 1812.

It is best if you are not in a rush because if you are, you will miss the great peacefulness that this area brings to the soul. Instead of following Route 33 as it heads south down to Tilghman Island, continue to land's end and what is left of the steamboats' dock. Get out of your auto and walk out on the landing, which is still waiting for the bygone days to return. The dock and the massive pilings are mute testimony to the activity which once made this spot a swirling, swarm of families with their little ones, young lovers holding

hands, older folks smiling into each other's eyes, all happy to be on their way, not to Claiborne, but to the resort by the sea.

Few opted to stay. When the train's whistle sounded, the call of the beaches and the open sea was so strong, everyone climbed aboard and left. Even the merry-go-round, put up in 1890, by Hode Taylor, and the nickelodeon that charged a nickel to watch a movie, were not able to keep folks there. They even tried running the film upside down and backwards, which made the cowboys chasing the Indians or the evil villain carrying off the damsel run backwards standing on their heads. Nothing helped. The Victorian niceties like box suppers, where guys bid for their favorite gal's picnic box, nor the hayrides, with the horses' jangling bells, not the berry picking, fish fires and oyster roasts, nor the canning factory or the oyster shucking plant and the produce packing company, not even the sight of the first gasoline powered log canoe, owned by a local fisherman, was help enough to keep Claiborne going. You get a lump in your throat as you look at the desolate scene. Your eyes go to the skyline searching for smoke drifting on the horizon signaling the arrival of a steamboat, but there are no more steamboats docking at Claiborne.

There used to be a bridge here when life was good and there were watermen, when boats, mostly log canoes, were built and the post office opened. But having a bridge did not guarantee that mail would come through in spite of dark of night, etc., and it seldom did. The bridge was another of the problems vexing Claiborne. It was not high enough to allow the boats to pass under and since it didn't have a draw, those with high cabins had to wait till low tide to get to the other side.

A new bridge, erected in 1932, at Knapps Narrows on down the peninsula, that did allow two cars to pass, that did have a draw and a bridge house attended twenty-four hours a day, took away the last bit of reason to go to Claiborne. Not for long will the bridge lift; a new span, high and wide, is under construction at this crossing, claimed by the locals to be one of the busiest in America, even the whole world. Here, there are a couple fine eating places to sample fish and other Shore delicacies and lots of antique emporiums.

Artists hang out at the bridge with their easels set up, their arm extended with their thumb firm on the handle of their brush measuring the height of something in the distance. With the white sails of the skipjacks framed against the cobalt blue sky, it is truly a celestial place for the painter. Half of the skipjacks call this island home, the others are down in Somerset County.

This Bay peninsula, called the Bay Hundred area because long ago when the English got to naming things they did it after their home tradition. "Hundreds," in the old English system, meant the area contained ten families or ten estates or could raise ten fighting men. There are more than ten families there now. It is surprising how many homes are there and how many boats, boats, boats. You see more boats than houses, every yard has two, maybe three, along with a truck or two.

Below the fishing village of Tilghman one is back to the heart of the Shore, where the beat of Easton and St. Michaels, the tourist towns, cannot be heard. The land is flat and low with a few stands of trees bordering the fields. It is a silent place where birds circle high above or wander the fields, where water wraps around you, where vestiges of the past are evident. You seldom pass another car as you drive along the road in this place apart.

The island remains the same as it has always been and there is no reason to believe that it will change much, and you are thankful for that, and for all that makes Talbot County a special place to visit.

USEFUL INFORMATION

Wye Mill. March-December, Saturday-Sunday, 11am-4pm. Donation.

Wye Oak, Wye Oak State Park, Wye Mills. Sunrise-sunset.

Wye Church, Wye Mills. Mid April-November, Tuesday-Saturday, 10am-3pm; Sunday, 1-4pm. Sunday services 11am.

Historical Society of Talbot County, 25 South Washington Street, Easton. Tuesday-Saturday, 10am-4pm; Sunday, 1-4pm. Closed Monday and Sunday January-March. Admission.

Academy of the Arts, Harrison and South Streets, Easton. Monday-Friday, 10am-4pm; Saturday, 1-4pm.

Third Haven Friends Meeting House, 405 South Washington Street, Easton.

St. Mary's Square Museum, "The Green", St. Michaels. May-October, Saturday-Sunday, 10am-4pm.

Chesapeake Bay Maritime Museum, St. Michaels Harbor, Maritime Road, St. Michaels. Summer, daily, 10am-5pm; January-March, Saturday-Sunday, 10am-4pm; rest of year, daily, 10am-4pm. Admission.

Oxford Museum, Morris and Market Streets, Oxford. Weekends. April-October 15, Friday-Saturday, 2-5pm. Donation.

Oxford-Bellevue Ferry, North Morris Street and the Strand. May-Labor Day, Monday-Friday, 7am-9pm; Saturday-Sunday, 9am-9pm. Labor Day-April, Monday-Friday, 7am-sunset; Saturday-Sunday, 9am-sunset. Closed Christmas-February. Toll.

For information and guides on Easton, St. Michaels and Oxford write: Talbot County Chamber of Commerce, P.O. Box 1366, 805 Goldsborough Street, Easton, Maryland 21601, or phone (301) 822-4606.

CAROLINE COUNTY

THE GREEN GARDEN COUNTY

CAROLINE COUNTY

Caroline County calls herself the "Green Garden County." If you look up the word green in the dictionary, the first description is "akin to grow." Garden is described in Webster's as "akin to enclosure...a plot of ground where herbs, fruits, flowers or vegetables are cultivated," and that's what folks do in Caroline County, they GROW and do it well.

Caroline has her heart in the right place, the center of the Delmarva Peninsula. She is a wedge of land bordered on the east by the state of Delaware, on the south by Talbot County and on the west by Queen Anne's. The bounty of her fertile soil is advertised "YOU PICK" or "WE PICK." This county is where the sweet juice of Caroline County melons is the nectar of the gods.

Far away from the madding crowds (sorry trite, but right), she is "big enough to serve you, small enough to know you," so say the Caroline County Commissioners. Caroline is truly a perfection of unsullied picturesque landscapes populated by sturdy, prideful, straight-forward folks who savor, with delight, their land, this place apart.

There weren't any roads worth mentioning in Caroline County back in 1773 or anywhere else on the Shore. To cast your vote or pay your taxes you went on the trail of the lonesome pine astride the old gray mare to Queenstown in Queen Anne's County or Cambridge in Dorchester County. Many folks found this situation aggravating, exasperating and very inconvenient. A group of forward-looking men gathered together and prayed, not in the spiritual sense of the word, but by the English form of law, to the General Assembly of the Province. Their prayer was a request to have a new county formed from Dorchester and Queen Anne's which they believed would prove to be a great convenience. (Typical English understatement.) The prayer was answered and Caroline County was born.

The ancestor for whom she is named was a sister of Frederick Calvert, the last of the Lords Baltimore. She was also the wife of Sir Robert Eden, the Royal Governor of the Province of Maryland. Remember, this was the New World owned by England and ruled by a king.

This spot was, apparently, still called Pig Point when Captain Zabdiel Potter settled there around 1730. He erected a "manor" at the upper reaches of the Choptank River where he believed commerce would be heavy. He was correct! Although, narrow at the mouth, the river was very deep allowing oceangoing vessels taking cargo to and from England and France to pass up and down with regularity.

"Potter Hall," as his estate became known, is still standing, albeit some additions, the kitchen section is authenticated as 1730 while the rest of the telescope-type brick house has been much altered. Captain Potter's brass knocker still adorns a rear door. Little is known about old Zabdiel but that he first settled Pig Point and that his grandson, Nathaniel, was a founding father of the College of Medicine at Johns Hopkins University in Baltimore.

A warehouse and a couple of homes were already there when a temporary seat of government was set up at Pig Point. (Pig Point, where in the "New World" did that name pig come from? Wasn't this area settled by the English? You could suppose that they might have dignified the Point by a good English moniker, say Swine Point.)

114

This county seat was a place of great importance then. The court would be in session at Melville's warehouse only when hogsheads of tobacco were not being weighed, stamped and stored for shipment--it was ordered by the court. (There's that name again, hog. Hogsheads have nothing to do with hogs, swine, or pigs, they are wooden barrels.)

Before the Revolution, people used tobacco as money. Talk about inconvenience! Imagine rolling a hogshead of tobacco into the grocery, you know, three crisp leaves for two eggs, several hogsheads for the rent. This was exactly what was happening. No paper money was allowed in the colonies. Folks were getting crotchety about having their pockets full of tiny pieces of shredded tobacco leaves. Cigarettes hadn't been thought of yet, so they prayed again.

They prayed to be allowed to print paper money hopefully backed by something of worth, but the Royal Proprietor of Maryland refused. Lots of trouble grew out of this refusal. The colonists insisted that they have the same rights enjoyed by men living in England. (Forget women, they had no rights at all.)

Charles Calvert came over from Great Britain and stopped at Annapolis where all had a high old time with a royal salute, toasts of rum, bonfires, dancing in the streets and lots of lavish parties, parties, parties. Charles Calvert was in no way distracted by these attempts to gain his favor. He did finally allow paper money to be printed in the colonies. He didn't come across the ocean for that; he came to change things, and he did. The Royal Proprietor had been happily collecting duty on tobacco being shipped in lieu of rents owed on the land.

Lord Baltimore put a stop to that and began collecting his own rent through local agents. His rent revenues totaled far more than the duty on tobacco ever had. (You see, in the end, real estate is always preferable to speculating in futures.) He took control of the government from the colonists by making the proprietor not dependent for his paycheck on the vote of the assembly. With this deathblow, all the power was removed from the American colonies. Baltimore sailed back to jolly ol' England patting himself on the back for his statesmanship.

This all took place in 1732 long before the American Revolution, but you can see smoke on the horizon. (To use a tried and true phrase.) Tobacco stayed the major export but smart folks were developing a more diversified economy. (Always be diversified. Any good stockbroker will tell you that.) Skilled craftsmen made goods which merchants sold at a profit. Corn and wheat became important exports. Livestock grew fat on the corn and the people of the West Indies grew fat on the salted beef. In the wetlands of the southern Eastern Shore lumber was cut and mills built. The lumber was used to build boats, houses, barns and docks. People kept coming and everything kept growing. The Shore hosted sailing ships from the far-flung ports of the world. The Maryland Assembly began creating counties and Caroline was one of them.

From 1682 until 1732 the boundary lines of Caroline County were in constant dispute. The Duke of York made a special grant of the Delaware section to William Penn. Proprietary Maryland had a fit. This dispute was eventually settled when it was decided to have the land surveyed. The thirty-eighth parallel established Maryland's northern border which then made it necessary to find the line, the middle point, that forms the eastern border of Caroline County.

Meanwhile the disagreement over the permanent location of the county seat raged on. One group wanted Bridgetown, now Greensboro, to be the permanent seat of government, not Pig Point. Those who already had the temporary seat wanted to have it made permanent. The "Bridgeers" felt the name, Pig Point, lacked dignity. (Again, lacked dignity! That classic British under-statement.) They had a point though, but their point was not taken and by Act of Assembly, in 1790, Pig Point became the county seat. Four acres of land were selected and purchased for the paltry sum of seven dollars an acre. The area was named Edenton by decree of the court. Everyone kept right on calling it Pig Point until a real courthouse was built.

By this time the court was meeting in a brick building presumed to be the old Brick Hotel which later burned. It took twenty years to get the courthouse erected. When it was ready, the officeholders were loathe to take up residence. They liked the hotel's room service and all the facilities. The court had to pass a law to force the Registrar of Wills, the Clerk of the Court, the Sheriff, as well as his deputies to move in. If they didn't, they were to be fined fifteen pounds. They all moved in immediately. At the same time the letter "E" was dropped from Edenton--Denton!

No sooner had things settled down than war, not between the court and their officeholders but, between the constituents and the Crown began. Colonel William Richardson was Caroline County's only hero of the Revolutionary War and is spoken of later in connection with the town known as American Corner.

As was true of many counties on Maryland's Eastern Shore, who did not have a border fronting on the Chesapeake Bay, the War of 1812 came and went with little notice, except for support of the cause.

The Civil War was a little different. In 1863, a company of Union soldiers were celebrating the fourth of July by shooting skyrockets high into the sky when one went awry. Behind what used to be Mr. Blackerton's store was a "rum shop" (presumption is that a "rum shop" was a liquor store or a brewery). The upper portion of this two-story structure was used to store flax and cotton.

As you might guess, this frame building with alcohol and dry goods inside went up with the first sparks from the rockets and took the rest of the town with it. This is why there are no eighteenth century buildings in downtown Denton.

Tobacco flourished for a while after the Revolutionary War. Farmers got rich and gave up the thrifty life and began living as their financial condition warranted. Three-story brick houses with eighteen-inch-thick walls, gabled roofs and large wings were very popular. When these mansions were completed,

they were often used for parties--any excuse would do. Gaiety was the watchword of the day.

It was not altogether fun and games. Children had to be taught their ABC's at home. There was weaving, then spinning, then making clothes. The mistress of the house tended to a few of these chores, but most were done by the slaves. Although in Caroline County there were fewer slaves than there were in the other counties on the Shore.

The master of the household rode the fields to keep check on the overseer. They ate well--game, fresh fish, succulent oysters, muskrat. (Yes muskrat, a delicacy on the Shore.) The orchards supplied fresh fruit and the kitchen garden burst forth with delectable veggies. Peaches, one of the most abundant of the fruits, were preserved into jam, but lots ended up in copper pots and became fine brandy. No one was concerned with moonshining then.

To dress for dinner was the occasion to "doll up." Linen shirts with ruffles and flourishes, fancy brocaded waistcoats hugged the body and silk stockings, low cut black patent leather shoes with shiny buckles made the men look dandy.

Not to be outdone by their "dandy" husbands, the wives dressed to the teeth. (Sorry trite, but right.) Tiny feet were slipped into high-heeled shoes and topped by bright-colored, floor-length, satin gowns with low, as low dared, necklines.

This was not only true of Caroline County but most of the world in the early 1800s. Not everyone lived so elegantly, however. Lots lived on farms, not to be confused with plantations. Their entertaining was done in the kitchen by the warmth of the hearth. They did not "change" for dinner, nor were their clothes silk. These sturdy, enduring, "common" people are the ancestors of those who populate Caroline County today. The "quality," the aristocrats of those early days are mostly unknown. Their mansions have tumbled down, their graves grown over with weeds and the names on the markers unreadable. A few of the old homesteads were kept in repair. They didn't all tumble down and Caroline still has some, if you care to nose around.

During this time, religion came to Caroline County. At first the Methodists did not convince as many Caroline Countians as they did others on the Shore, that to be a Methodist was to be "saved." The Methodist church got going in the parlor of William Frazier's home which came to be known as the "Church Room." This first gathering led to Frazier Chapel, built before 1865, at what is now the town of Preston, and known later as Bethesda Chapel.

There is a story about this first church. It seems that a circuit rider came by and as he approached the settlement, he decided that when he passed through town he would sing a hymn. If he was invited to stop, he would assume that this was a sign from the Almighty that he should organize a church right there in Preston. They did and he did.

As is not unusual, the name before Preston was Snow Hill. There was another Snow Hill on the Eastern Shore, as you know. So when they found this out, the name was changed to Preston.

Apparently Preston attracted the devout because soon there was a Lutheran church where services for many, many years were spoken in German and in English, both. Nothing happened besides church suppers and festivals until the railroad came in 1890. Even then not much happened.

The Quakers got to town before the Methodists and had a meetinghouse outside of Denton. Over the Tuckahoe River Bridge, from Denton, stands the meetinghouse solemn and silent. Sagging in the middle and in need of a good paint scraper, she waits for the yearly meeting the Quakers still hold. There is a historical marker that tells you the meetinghouse was built in 1802 by the members of the Society of Friends who had been Nickolites, a sect that was organized in Caroline County. The building, once a Friends school, was rented to the Dunkards (Dunkards, members of the Church of the Brethren, originally a German Baptist denomination, were conscientious objectors) and used as a place for

religious meetings of black persons. If you want to go inside, go to the Electric Cooperative on whose grounds the old church stands and get the key at the office. (Only on the Eastern Shore do you run into such instructions.)

The Episcopalians got there before anyone else, even the Quakers. After all weren't the early settlers all members of the Church of England? There are records to substantiate that they were here fifty years earlier than the Quakers and Puritans. A problem crept up when the guns of the Revolution began firing. The priests were expected "to be loyal and bear allegiance to the government of England." This oath, if not taken, forced the clergy to return to the homeland immediately. Most went back, abandoning the parishes. Then the Church got this idea of the "forty pound tax." A tax to be paid in forty pounds of tobacco for the support of the ministers and for such funds needed to build or repair chapels. Folks simply didn't take to this proposal since the men of the cloth were already getting sixty dollars a year. Many of the parishioners deserted the Church to become gospel-singing Methodists.

Preston was known as the "biggest little town in the USA" during the 1920s. This feat was accomplished because of the foresight and ingenuity of its citizens. So says Howard Harris in the commentary booklet published to celebrate Caroline County's 200th anniversary.

He goes on to tell you Preston holds the record for a small town in the number of dwelling houses moved from one place to another. (Again, this moving of houses by truck along the highways of the Eastern Shore is so common as to attract no attention whatsoever from other drivers.) The old school building's four sections can be spotted all over Preston, if you know what to look for.

Besides holding the record for house moving, it is a matter of record that Preston led the nation in the number who paid taxes. Preston was the first town of its size to pave the sidewalks with concrete, add a sewer system and install electric street lights. To continue Preston had a water system which could supply

a town three times its size. The first tomato cannery, the first sweet potato storage house, the first gasoline powered farm tractor was bought by a resident and the first canned goods were packed in Preston.

As you are probably aware by now, most villages in those days, that made a go of it, were along water of some kind, be it stream, creek, river or inlet. If you're near water, then you need to be able to get across. You need a bridge or a ferry.

The only bridge across the Choptank was at Greensboro. The only bridge across the Upper Tuckahoe was at Hillsboro. The only bridge across Marshyhope Creek, a tributary of the Choptank River, was at Federalsburg. These towns are on the map today.

To travel a mile or two then was to drive twenty miles today. To help the folks get around, the County maintained ferries at midpoint between the towns and the bridges. The ferry ride cost you 8 cents for foot passengers, 16 cents for four-legged animals, two-wheel carriages, horse and passenger, 25 cents, four-wheel phaeton (the touring car of the day) with horse and passenger, 75 cents, and black cattle, 12 cents. This rate was for "foreigners." The residents of the County rode free.

Another way to survive as a community was to have a general store. The general store was everything to everyone, the hostess with the mostest, the beginning and the end for the community that lived in the vicinity of this emporium of everything. The general stores on the Eastern Shore were, the same in the Upper Chesapeake Region as on the Southern Eastern Shore, the center of activity.

Steamboats represented high times for many counties of the Shore that were on the Bay and the rivers, and Caroline had her share. Vaudeville shows were the entertainment aboard and were so, so popular. A pair of obese men, the combined weight of these two Johns, both had the same first name, was over 700 pounds. They were packing them in (sorry trite, but right) by performing "The Fat Man's Club" on the steamers. These two vaudevillians decided to open their own theater on dry land where they didn't have to squeeze their blubber to pass along the narrow companionways.

They bought a farm at Kennel's Landing which, because of them, is now known as Two Johns. They redid the old place, turning it into a spectacular edifice of entertainment. The assembly hall was where they put on their act and an observation tower on the roof, like a widow's walk, was where the two watched for the steamboats from Baltimore. Two Johns became a regular Port of Call. The acts in the hall were only for gentlemen (nothing is mentioned about the ladies). The "gentlemen" were mostly farmers.

Now if you were a town not on the water or near a bridge or a ferry or a general store, you were a town no more, unless you had a plan.

Then as now, there are planned communities. Once, long ago, a town named Ridgely, near Frazier's Chapel, was a planned community, planned by Reverend Greenbury W. Ridgely. The story goes that a "body of men from Philadelphia heard the call of the city," and the Maryland and Baltimore Land Association was formed and went forth with a dream of "planning a city," a dreamland that would unite the railroad and the Choptank River. A large, very large, amount of land was purchased in 1867 by the well-to-do preacher with the understanding that this paradise would be named after him.

A survey was made and, also, a most marketable map in full color with drawings of trees and parks and fountains and stores and such other attractive things which, it was hoped, would bring buyers. The map not only covered the present limits of the town, but extended the railroad to Ridgely because the town was to have a waterfront with shipyards and manufacturing plants. So far, the railroad had only reached Greensboro, but the group promised to supply the ties, and the railroad was built. Now here you have a town with a fine city plan, on the water, with transportation, all anyone could wish for.

Building began and continued until the bills came in. No money seemed to be available to pay them. A clamor rose like a tidal wave and the painters, the carpenters, the lumber dealers and the construction workers all demanded to be paid. Well, they weren't. Left, were two parks, a vacant hotel, a train station and two stores.

The present town of Ridgely follows exactly the map of 1867. (How did the present town come to be, you ask?) Two entrepreneurs arrived to engage themselves in real estate. They tried Porter's Landing, but when the word about the defunct association got to them, they rushed over to Ridgely. Floods of advertisements were mailed across the country. The advertisements spoke of the fabulous advantages of Ridgely with its railroad and the beautiful streets and parks. Settlers from as far away as Michigan and Wisconsin flooded in to buy a piece of paradise.

Ridgely went on to become the home of the Armour Plant which was one of the largest preserving factories in the world. They imported "foreign" workers and advertised that the plant and the workers and the workers' homes had "approved sanitary conditions." Ridgely was a company town and, as always, you owed your life to the company store. (You've heard that before.)

Swing Company Factory, where tomatoes were canned, used exclusively the tomatoes from their own acreage. This company also had a factory which made crates, baskets and strawberry cups (?) which "gained a reputation" throughout Maryland and New Jersey. Ridgely still has a vegetable packing plant, a feed company (chicken feed, one presumes), a shirt factory, a beverage plant and a fish hatchery.

As is true of the counties all over the Eastern Shore, it is true of Caroline. Towns have been lost. They are referred to in yellowed paper found in the archives of the county courthouses or in a trunk in someone's attic or wherever old things grow older.

It seems that Caroline has a mystery town, a ghost town of sorts. A dot on the state highway map showed, and still does, a town located precisely three miles

127

east of Route 16 in south central Caroline County named American Corner, but no town exists so says James C. Wilfong, Jr., in a piece published in The News Leader, Laurel, Maryland, on August 11, 1966.

"When memorial services for Charles Dickenson were held near Preston on May 29, 1966, 160 years after his death at the hands of Andrew Jackson, some among those attending must have found interest in a road directional sign a few feet from the site. It reads American Corner three miles.

"For many years the State Roads Commission maps, published annually, have painstakingly shown American Corner precisely three miles east of Route 16, placing it in the south-central part of Caroline County. As a point of curiosity an attempt was made to determine the origin of the strange name. The editor of the Caroline County News and Farmer who had spearheaded the efforts to locate the lost site of Dickenson's original grave could offer no facts concerning American Corner's origins. He cited two references, however, possibly treating it. Unfortunately, they offered little help.

"A call to Enoch Pratt's Maryland Room confirmed only that this was something of a mystery town, believed to be perhaps one hundred years old, at the most and very small in its extent - possibly consisting of five homes with a population of about a dozen.

"The Baltimore Sun's version of The Washington Star's Action Line told little more, other than that some further mystery was attached to the correct spelling of the name. Some sources, it was stated, called it American Corners, plural.

"A telephone call to the U.S. Census Bureau in Suitland brought an amused response. The town name was repeated and the information specialist said in an aside that she'd never heard of it. This was not surprising, since a great many native Marylanders seemed equally uninformed on the point. She was obliging, though, and left the line to check her records. She returned, laughing pleasantly. 'It doesn't have any population,' she said. We questioned this closely. 'No,' she replied, 'we show it as a "rural area, population zero."'

"Another thought occurred: if recorded history fails to solve perplexing mysteries such unenlightening sources can always be brushed aside conveniently. Theories are not as authentic but they can be pleasantly arrived at. Sometimes they might even hold water.

"The thought crossed the mind that here a dozen or more citizens might officially escape taxes in all their myriad forms and live blithely and completely oblivious to 20th Century civilization with all of its other annoyances -- serene in the knowledge that a great statistical arm of the U.S. Government said simply that they did not exist.

"But we have seen a roadside sign on Route 16 and we had a store of maps down through the years that said without qualification that there was, indeed, a town of American Corner, Md.

"The key to the mystery could possibly be contained in another roadside sign, a mile north of the other. Here, at the intersection of Wilkins Bridge Road and Route 16, a historical marker honors the memory of Colonel William Richardson, who lived and lies buried at Gilpin Point, a mile west of here. Its inscription tells that the colonel was a great man in these parts and that he lived a long life--born in 1735 and died in 1825. Possibly whatever he did in the way of saving the Eastern Shore from Tories was performed at a point known today as American Corner."

Actually there are at least twelve homes in American Corner and a road sign with the name American Corner. Where the facts published in this piece, "Caroline County Mystery Town," came from one can only guess that this misinformation is from a writer who did not do his own research. The piece is left because it is interesting and because this writer believed every word until American Corner turned up right where it is supposed to be.

Colonel Richardson, known as the "father" of Caroline County, died in 1825. He is credited with having introduced the bill creating the County. The colonel was in charge of Maryland's Flying Camp, a mobile unit with the ability to change location with speed. In 1777 when Philadelphia was threatened, the colonel moved the Treasury to Baltimore. Colonel Richardson did a great deal to rid the Shore of Tories. He lived at Gilpin Point, only three miles from American Corner.

Joshua Barney, a successful privateer during the Revolutionary War was captured by the British in 1781 and taken to Mill Prison in Plymouth, England. He escaped and, by chance, met the colonel and his friend at the home of a minister where they were staying while waiting to find a way back to America.

Barney described the two men in his journal as two farmers. It was a problem to find a ship willing to take the "farmers" back to the New World when a war was raging. If the colonel would engage a fishing boat, Barney agreed to dress up in fisherman's clothes and take them across the English Channel to France. From there it would be no problem getting a ship back to the "Shore." You see, the French were neutral, so a ship flying the flag of France would be able to pass through the blockade and enter the Bay, maybe.

On the trip across the always angry waters of the English Channel, Richardson suffered mal de mer and the boat was captured and they were all hauled back to Plymouth. Barney was returned to Mill Prison, but luckily his companions were released. (How they returned to the Eastern Shore is never revealed. This information seems to this author to be a rather important part of the story. Oh well, Richardson managed it somehow because he is buried on his estate at Gilpin Point.) Colonel Richardson's tomb, almost covered with vines, and the crumbling walls of the coral rock wall that surrounded his huge estate are all that is left. The coral to build this wall was ballast on Richardson's sloop, the Omega, who sailed the shipping lanes of the West Indies.

Tuckahoe Creek, a lazy stream, where the green Tuckahoe grass lining its bank is reflected on the still surface, meets the Choptank River at Gilpin Point and is a lovely spot to reflect on men like Richardson. It is much smaller than the mighty Choptank which runs forty miles through Caroline County.

If you would like to row up the lazy river in the noonday sun, you can rent a canoe during July and August at Tuckahoe State Park. If you don't want to paddle a canoe, you can peddle your bike along the three miles of surfaced trail or paddle your feet through the Adkin's Arboretum. Your trail will lead past five hundred acres of flora and fauna, all indigenous to Maryland. Campsites, picnic tables and boats are available. Besides Tuckahoe Park, there is Martinak, a state park where you fish in the same lake the Indians used when they were there. At least it appears that the high ground could have been the site of a village. A treaty with the Indians, in 1669, granted a three-square-mile reservation to the Algonquin Choptanks for an annual rent of six beaver skins.

The social life in the County during these times was lively and exciting, but hardly ever lavish except for the "plantation set" who did it up a bit. They visited Annapolis when the assembly was in session or went to Denton when the court met. The brick hotel was the favored spot to stop unless you were house guests at one of the plantations during a fox hunt.

At one of these plantation affairs Andrew Jackson met the hostess' brother, Charles Dickenson. This young man was considered by most to be a highly strung, impetuous and imprudent lawyer who helped form the Caroline County Militia in the Revolutionary War.

Among other expensive habits, Dickenson was fond of breeding fine stallions. Upon the occasion of his meeting again with "Old Hickory" in Tennessee, there was a heated discussion about the merits of Jackson's favorite steed, Trurton, and a steed owned and bred by this young lawyer. It was deemed prudent by Andy Jackson to place a forfeit against the possibility of Dickenson's horse being scratched from the planned race. This happened, and when the paper tendered as collateral proved to be worthless, Jackson called out young Dickenson.

The two men faced each other on the "field of honor," a piece of land at Harrison's Mill on the Red River in Kentucky. It was decided that in all fairness, Dickenson would be first since Jackson, showing off,

had, with one shot, just cut the string that was hanging from a tree with an apple attached. Dickenson fired, Jackson grinned, then he brushed aside a bit of dust on his shirt from the bullet which had apparently only grazed him. "Old Hickory" took aim, squeezed the trigger, and...the gun jammed at half cock. Jackson muttered a curse, took aim again, squeezed the trigger and shot Dickenson, cutting an artery. (A terminal wound in those days, probably any day.) As it turned out, Jackson was actually hit in the chest and had two ribs broken. Hickory is a tough wood and Jackson a tough man, who was only laid up for a few weeks. (Oh, men and honor.)

Duels, on the "field of honor" continued to plague Caroline County's men. James Gordon Bennett, the well-known editor and owner of the New York Herald, and Fred May, playboy, polo fan, world traveler and explorer, fought a duel over a woman. A woman scorned is a sight to behold and Fred May could not stand to behold his sister who had been jilted by Bennett. The field was outside Marydel. It was a sight to see. The dueling parties, or rather two dueling parties, were a group of young men dressed to the teeth (sorry trite, but right), who carried blankets to be used for wrapping the dead. (Maybe shroud would have been a better word than blanket, but at any rate there were no dead.) Neither being of the ilk of Jackson, they both missed and that was the end of it. All of this notoriety didn't help Marydel much more than did the arrival of the railroad in 1866.

Marydel's claim to fame, other than hosting duels, is the crown stone placed by Charles Mason and Jeremiah Dixon at the spot where Maryland and Pennsylvania meet. It was put there about one hundred years before Marydel existed. Each of the six hundred pound stones came from England and Maryland's is one of fifteen. Today the stone marks the division between Delaware and Maryland rather than Pennsylvania. The town was named after the stone, as you can tell, "mary" for Maryland and "del" for Delaware.

Marydel was another planned community whose plans didn't fully materialize. When she was formed, there were about forty homes, a cannery and a mill. The crown

stone is still there about a mile out of this small hamlet.

If you have read Volume I of <u>Maryland's Eastern Shore, A Place Apart</u>, you already know about the infamous Patty Cannon and her partner, Joe Johnson, and their goings-on. Bridgetown was the home of Marcy Fountain, a cohort of Patty and Joe. A slave peddler, he was accused of selling bodies for money. It was well known that he dealt openly with Negroes brought to him by more squeamish types who feared discovery. Fountain would sell his "merchandise...South to Georgia," as it was put. "South to Georgia" was a phrase that caused the black man to turn white with fear.

This powerful man kept his salable humans in the cellar and politics on his mind. He had influence and money, a winning combination for any politician. Happy to say, he never held office in Caroline County or elsewhere.

Of all the small places in Caroline, Greensboro is probably largest. Walking along the main street, you stand out as a "foreigner." In a town where everyone knows everyone, no exceptions, a stranger on Main Street provokes curiosity. Heads turn and if you smile, they will smile back. The restaurant, the only one in town, has a sign in the window, "shore good cookin'" and it "shore" is.

Around the corner you are struck by the sight of a log cabin crammed in among the early 1900s homes. It's just sitting there in a bower of flowers with a green-clipped lawn and a brick path protected from intruders by a chain across the entrance. (Ignore this. There is no lock, simply a latch that's easy to unfasten.) The brick path is lined with flowers, the kind you remember from childhood--bright orange poppies, hollyhocks, day lilies, asters and a purple clematis climbs the rail fence.

There is no one around to ask where the log cabin came from or how it got there. (A good guess is that it was brought from somewhere else, nothing to it as you know.) A thought, which proved to be true, is that it was moved from a field outside Preston. You follow the red brick path around back and there is a **SIGHT!** You stare at what appears to be a bench, but is gray metal, no back and is kind of low to the ground. You ask yourself, what is it? Not a bench? Odd material for a resting place, this gray metal box with huge nails, like roofing nails, studding the top--nails--is it a coffin? Could be, and is. You don't sit down, but you peak through a hole along the top side and you see nothing but leaves and a bit of trash inside, no body. The mystery is not cleared by asking one of the octogenarians walking by carrying her bag of groceries. She tells you that the town historian, who knows everything about the history of Greensboro, is the undertaker and that the parlor is just a couple houses up the street. News does not travel fast in town, apparently, because the undertaker died two years ago you are told when you reach the funeral home. If you really want to know, you go to town hall. No one there knows either, but they tell you that the man who lives in the house next door does.

You seek him out, no problem just knock on the door, most locals are delighted to be asked about their home towns. It is a coffin, the coffin of Charles Dickenson, the man whom Andrew Jackson killed in the duel. Well, it seems the coffin was dug up in a field five hundred yards from the historical marker honoring Charles Dickenson along the road to Preston. The marker tells you that Charles Dickenson was born in Caroline County in 1780, that he moved to Foxley Hall in Easton in 1795, that Dickenson read law under Judge Marshall, and that he met Andrew Jackson (unfortunately) who was traveling across the Eastern Shore to the United States Congress. Dickenson moved to Nashville, Tennessee. You find out that he was killed by Jackson in a duel, and that his body was returned to Caroline County by Truxton (one name only), faithful Negro servant, and that his lead coffin was found five hundred yards from this marker which you already know. But you didn't know that it was found December 1, 1965, almost one hundred and sixty years later. This explains why the material the coffin is made of looks so strange. One doesn't see many lead coffins these days. You wonder why there are no bones inside, but there are not.

Right next door is the Goldsborough House, the Historical Society of Caroline County has plans to open a restaurant in the home which is late 1800s and not historic, only noted in respect that a town personage lived there. Judge Laird Goldsborough was Adjutant General of the Philippines, authored their first constitution, and his descendants distinguished themselves in public service. (One wonders if this town can support two restaurants.)

Greensboro will forever be immortalized by the following poem recited by Bessie Edwards and published in History of Caroline County, compiled by the Queen Anne's Historical Society.

"A RHYME OF BYGONE YEARS.

Listen, good people, and you shall hear
The story of many a bygone year.
Reaching back to the days of yore
When Indians wandered on Eastern Shore.
Even to sixteen-hundred eight (1608)
When Smith explored the Eastern state.

Once more, five years ere Baltimore came
Claiborne exploring found again
Metapeake, Nanticoke, and Choptank,
Lurking in forests deep and dank.

Sixteen-hundred sixty-nine (1669)
This is the year in which I find
Governor Calvert--Charles by name
Granted the Indians certain claim
To lands. These they could call their own
A "Reservation". The Indians home.
Six beaver skins they yearly sent
To the Lord Proprietor for rent.

For sixteen-hundred eighty-three (1683)
An interesting chapter see.
To the home of William Troth one day
A drunken Indian chanced to stray,
He, both with tomahawk and gun,
Tried for Troth's life--Then away he run.

The trial came, Court judgment sent
The Indian far. 'Twas, "Banishment".
On the Court records e'en to-day is
The noted trial of Poh Poh Caquis.

Years passed. In seventeen-hundred-four (1704)
The rising power of the white man bore
The Red man backward through forest glade,
'Twas then the Nanticoke Treaty was made.
So civilization rose like the tide
And the Indians were scattered far and wide.

As time rolled on the traffic grew,
And so, in seventeen thirty-two (1732)
The government granted the people right
To plot a town on Greensboro's site,
A bridge across the river was thrown,
Accordingly it was called Bridgetown.

Twenty acres in Dorchester lay
Per acre twenty-four shillings they pay,
Twenty more by Queen Anne were given
Shillings per acre, twenty-seven,
And the purchasers paid for years,--oh many
The Lord Proprietor a tax of one penny.
Such is the story I tell to you
Of Greensboro,--Seventeen thirty-two. (1732)

In fifty-six Arcadians came (1756)
The Huguenot French well known to fame,
Who knows but some fair Evangeline
At Bridgetown crossing was oftimes seen.

Then just before the birth of our Nation
Caroline County was given foundation,
Made from Queen Anne and Dorchester--
Talbot also formed part of her.
Caroline Calvert the name was for,
Wife of Lord Eden, the Governor
Who served the King on Eastern Shore
The year of our Lord, seventeen-seventy-four. (1774)

Soon was the Revolution here
With its midnight ride of Paul Revere.
Soldiers were gathering by the score,
And Caroline added one company more.

What found we then in a soldiers pack?
What carried he in his haversack?
One half pound powder; a bag of ball;
Two pounds of lead, Nor was this all,
A cartridge box filled with cartouch;
A powder horn. What more could you wish
Except his flintlock with trigger set,
And barrel pointed by bayonet.
Some of the bravest no doubt were found,
Carrying guns from old Bridgetown
Then, they made the English run,
Just as yesterday they made the Hun.

Seventeen hundred ninety-one (1791)
War was over. Peace had come.
The State Assembly authorized
That Bridgetown be reorganized.
The old town stood as heretofore
But added one hundred acres more
Purchased from lands on the Western bank
Where the bridge led over the old Choptank.
There on an Indian summer day
Old Bridgetown was laid away.
The new town born was called I trow
By its present name of Greensboro.
Both records and folk-lore prove I ween
That the town was named for one Valentine Green.

You know the rest,--How Greensboro through
The following century steadily grew,
How in eighteen-eight (1808) a new bridge was thrown
Over the Choptank. The old was down,
How eighteen-sixteen (1816) Public School
And free education became the rule,
Then at a date that has not appeared
A Presbyterian Church was reared.

Later Episcopal and M. E.
Were added to Greensboro's family tree.
In eighteen-twenty-five (1825) you get
Your medicine from Dr. Rousset.
In 1880 a newspaper. Guess?
Why of course the Greensboro Free Press.
Railroad, factories, canneries came.
Now Greensboro is known to fame.

Here's a toast. May her fame spread far and wide
Then, higher rise, like a Choptank tide.
And though in distant lands we roam
May we e'er be proud to call Greensboro--Home."

Of all the counties on Maryland's Eastern Shore, Caroline is the least known, the least visited, the last in line for the tourist, but she is the most American of them all.

You could call Caroline the "Parade County" instead of the "Green Garden County," which is how she is described in the tourism brochure. Any excuse for a parade in Caroline County will do. Mobs of people crowd the main street of Federalsburg for the "Anything Goes Day Parade," one of the biggest events in Federalsburg over the last decade. The volunteer fire department's carnival parade in the summer, the Halloween, Christmas and little league parades (all the teams in the County are in every parade), are to name a few.

The town of Federalsburg is known as "King Parade" with the lollapalooza being the "Anything Goes Day Parade," which lasts two days. The Federalsburg Jaycees and the Downtown Business Association do their part in organizing these festivities, but "Mr. and Mrs. Parade" (Ben and Betty Happersett) got it going. These parades are not small affairs, they include the biggest fire engines you've ever seen, all mostly gleaming silver and white rather than red and as long as a railroad car. Mostly, they are preceded by Cadillac convertibles, each with a "Queen" waving from the back deck. There is a "Queen" for every age group of the little league, even the preschool T-ball team. There are marching bands and majorettes, and every business in town has a float. The parade could put the big cities across the Bay Bridge to shame (Disney World excepted).

Federalsburg is a growing industrial city and the largest town in the County. Trucks started rolling in during the 1930s. The only railroad operating in the County is there. The city is ranked as the first among the state of Maryland's one hundred and fifty-four municipalities in taxable property for the 1981-1986 period. During this period new businesses began, and

141

have doubled in size. The reason for this expansion is that flooding, a major problem for years, was finally controlled.

Sailing ships don't call anymore, the wharfs along the Marshyhope are all gone, as are the livery stables, the two blacksmiths, the general stores, the Riverview Hotel, the Long and Short Department Store, but other establishments are still run by the same families. Ships like the clippers, the Richard Tull, the Eggleston Brown, the Mary Havilow, the Jacob Charles, the Pearl and the Annabelle were built in Federalsburg once, but no more. Two major supermarkets, a modern marina, tennis and basketball courts, beauty shops, a TV sales and service shop, insurance companies, a nice library and a radio station have replaced what was there.

If you read the Caroline County Times-Record, you will note that the circus is coming and folks are invited to watch the Big Top go up, a front page piece! The largest birdathon contest ever will put birders in competition, another front page piece, "Local Auduboners will join birders across the country, scanning the skies, bushes and water in a 24-hour marathon attempt to identify as many species as possible." Sponsors make pledges of anything from a nickel to two dollars, which helps finance the local chapter projects as well as the National Audubon Society activities. Then there is the page of news for the young which talks about the 4-H Center, Yosemite National Park is noted, a discussion on naturalization of foreigners, and about Charles Dickenson (not the dueler, but about the prominent family). There are games...Word Search, Gobble-De-Gook and a Mystery Message. They write about nature in Caroline County and how far it is to Boston, three hundred and ninety-six miles. What a marvelous way to get children use to reading the paper. The Washington Post would do well to take a look at this paper.

The little towns of Caroline have remained much the same except for Federalsburg, of course. Some have not remained a'tall. You do not see Bee Tree or Burrsville on the County or Maryland State Maps, although both were once there. Bee Tree (cute name) was called that because of the swarms of bees that inhabited

the place. You can understand why it might be deserted today even if once there was a school, at least a school commission was appointed in 1865, and in 1866 a new school was erected near Melville's Cross Roads, close by.

Burrsville and the adjoining villages of Union Corners and Punch Hall are believed to be related in some way, no one knows how. The name Burrsville was selected for the post office without asking anyone. Punch Hall was called that because runaway slaves crawled under a building, called a hall, and these fugitives had to be punched out with long poles. Others say the name came from a citizen by the name of Hall who ran an inn and sold strong drinks that made you punchy.

When Denton took its place as the seat of government, the county of Caroline finally had an identity. Denton could be described in many ways, but to say that it is homey says it best. Not much has changed in Denton since World War II. This pretty town still flies the flag on the fourth of July and decorates graves on Decoration Day, now called Memorial Day, but not in Denton. They stick to the familiar Decoration Day and most go to the cemetery to put fresh flowers on the graves, which is why that day was originally called Decoration Day. There is a Christian book store, the inevitable Dollar General Store, one restaurant and one traffic light in the two-block "downtown."

Both the Christian book store and Dollar General Store are popular on the Shore and show up in almost every town. We all know Christian book stores are inherently good places to work. You might be interested to know that an operation like the Dollar General Store, which is in business to sell and not to necessarily be a "good" place to work, offers its employees a future that few other retail businesses would even consider. As an employee of any of the thirteen hundred Dollar General Stores in twenty-three states, you have the opportunity to learn to read, take the GED (Graduate Equivalency Diploma) test and get your diploma, or if you are literate, teach someone else. This is an incredible program for a company to offer.

A little background on how this opportunity came about. The founder's great grandfather was killed in a Saturday night wrestling match in Macon County, Kentucky. He was only thirty-three years old and his son, J. L. Turner, a third grader, had to drop out of school to work the farm. He was the sole support for his mother and three younger brothers and sisters. Although he never received any more schooling, he managed to found the first Dollar General Store with his son, Cal. "JL" took Cal everywhere he went to "pencil store stock" (add and subtract). Cal went on to college, and together father and son ran a first-class discount, retail operation. This probably couldn't be pulled off in today's world. The Turner family and their accomplishment is mentioned because the author is very impressed with these folks and their desire to help their employees get the education necessary to survive in today's world. (This author never misses an opportunity to shop the Dollar General Store and never fails to get a bargain.)

The town hall in Denton resembles most others on the Shore. There is a first-class library and the old brick hotel is still standing, even after the fire that destroyed all the other structures in town. The courthouse sits majestically surrounded by green grass and benches along the sidewalk line the front. A nice spot to sit and enjoy the tranquility, if it's not a parade day. The huge round clock centered in the cupola atop the courthouse lets you know that time is not really standing still.

Local affairs have always occupied the residents of Denton. County politics are not taken lightly here. The townsfolk are deeply involved in issues of a local nature and can cause a fury of controversy that keeps the various factions of the Democratic Party boiling. Forget the Republicans--they are hardly noticeable. You will believe this when you see the large marble marker along the curb across from the courthouse which has engraved these words, "On this spot, September 5, 1938, stood Franklin Delano Roosevelt. It is the privilege of some of us to dream, and some of us to carry out the dreams of others." A maple tree shades the spot.

Caroline County is a family farm county with farming in four major areas--grain, dairying, truck gardening and raising poultry. This is the only county in the state that farms in all four major endeavors. A spinoff from farming is canning and that is still a growing industry, as is the manufacturing of shirt buttons, plastics and processing of chickens. The industrious residents have not missed a bet.

The farmers depend heavily on the Maryland Extension Service for advice on crops, livestock, products, marketing and farm management. The 4-H is the center of social life for the youngsters and continues to expand its activities. This organization has led in the development of youth into capable, sensitive and productive citizens. (Could use a 4-H in the big cities on the "other side," but alas, unless we dig up the downtown and plant corn...)

"Productive citizens," exactly what does that mean? In Caroline County it means the discipline dealing with what is good and bad and with moral duty and obligation. In Caroline County there is a commitment to the community by the young people, as well as to themselves.

At the county fair they crown the princess and prince of 4-H and award the much-sought-after blue ribbons. The young follow the 4-H motto, "to make the best better." Caroline County is a nice place for children to grow up. The lives of young and old alike center around the churches. The devout are thankful for the bounty of their land, and if you visit, you, too, will be thankful for the bounty of Caroline County.

USEFUL INFORMATION

Martinak State Park, Deep Shore Road off Route 404, Denton. Daily, 8am-4:30pm. For information write: Park Superintendent, Martinak State Park, Denton, Maryland 21629.

Tuckahoe State Park, 3 miles north of Hillsboro (off Route 404 on Eveland Road which intersects with Route 480). Open until sunset. For information write: Park Manager, Tuckahoe State Park, Route 1, P.O. Box 23, Queen Anne, Maryland 21657.

For information on Caroline County write: Tourism Council of the Upper Chesapeake, P.O. Box 66, Centreville, Maryland 21617.

Questions about Denton? Write: Denton Town Office, 13 North Third Street, Denton, Maryland 21629 or phone (301) 479-2050.

For information on boating, marinas, wharfs, fishing, lakes and ponds and where to get a license write: County Commissioners of Caroline County, P.O. Box 207, Denton, Maryland 21629, or phone (301) 479-0660.

KENT COUNTY

THE TEA PARTY COUNTY

KENT COUNTY

Kent County is enclosed by the high banks of the Sassafras River on the north, on the south by the splendid Chester River, a mile wide at its mouth, and on the west by the Chesapeake Bay, where all rivers on the Eastern Shore flow.

She is the second oldest county in Maryland, preceded only by St. Mary's. If St. Mary's County is the mother of Maryland, then Kent is the surrogate mother of Maryland's Eastern Shore.

The land is an area protected from the storms and floods that pester most Eastern Shore counties. The climate is gentle, the soil fertile, and because of this, the economy is largely agrarian. When Captain John Smith first explored the Upper Chesapeake, he noted the vast number of wild game and fish, all so true.

At one time, Kent encompassed all of the land east of the Bay and up through what is now the state of Delaware. She was named by feisty William Claiborne who settled Kent Island, now a part of Queen Anne's County. The name came from the maritime shire of Kent in Great Britain. (Wonder how the word shire lost out to county.)

From such an auspicious beginning, parts of Kent were absorbed by the formation of new counties until she

is now the smallest of them all. She may be the
smallest in size, but possibly the largest in history,
particularly the county seat, Chestertown.

Mr. Hortt Deringer, editor of the Kent County
News, "fears Chestertown could pickle itself in its own
history and become a museum."

The Kent Countians are fiercely proud of their
"firsts" and will tick them off for you if you are of a
mind to listen. The list is as follows: site of the
first settlement on the Eastern Shore which lasted
(Eastern Neck), first church on the mainland of the
Eastern Shore (the ruins can be seen when Church Creek
is at ebb tide), the terminus of the first turnpike in
America (Rock Hall), the first troops ordered out to
fight in the Revolutionary War (the militia), and the
first Maryland county to give the vote to women (1908 at
Still Pond's town election).

Washington College has so many firsts that it
deserves to have a paragraph all its own. Washington
College was the first institution of higher learning to
be granted a charter by the state of Maryland, the first
to hold a commencement for its graduates, and the first
to be named for George Washington with his express
consent which he gave in these words. "I am much
indebted for the honor conferred on me by giving my name
to the college at Chester." ("Town" hadn't been added
as yet.)

Captain James, Samuel and John Nicholson were a
famous trio. James, the first Commander-in-Chief of the
Continental Navy, held his position against the claims
of John Paul Jones that perhaps he, Jones, should be
commander. Samuel supervised the construction of Old
Ironsides and the U.S.S. Constellation. James also
served as John Paul Jones' lieutenant, on the Bon Homme
Richard, in the battle with the huge British ship,
Serapis. In addition, Samuel took the last naval
"prize" of the Revolution and four of his sons grew up
to be naval officers. John seems to have been
overlooked although he is listed as one of the three
brothers in The Eastern Shore of Maryland and Virginia
by Charles B. Clark. Clark fails to list John's deeds
unless they are mixed up with those of Samuel who seemed

154

to be everywhere. (The author is resistant to searching further for information on John.)

Alexander Murray of Chestertown, opened the first engagement with the infamous pirates of Tripoli who had been obliterating ships from the American Navy at a fast rate. He sailed into the Mediterranean and attacked a flotilla of seventeen gunboats and blockaded Tripoli's harbor for two months. His grandson became an admiral!

Captain Lambert Wickes gallantly commanded the Reprisal during the Revolutionary War and was responsible for Benjamin Franklin's safety enroute to France on a secret mission. Wickes was the first naval officer named by Congress, in 1776, to carry the American flag into European waters where he captured a British vessel. It was said of him by John Barney, the commander of the fledgling American Navy, "...one of the bravest men that ever existed." He was lost at sea when his ship went down off the banks of Newfoundland on its return from France.

Major Joseph Wickes, the patriarch of the family, was a man of breeding and refinement who settled on Eastern Neck Island in 1658 and built a manor home called "Wickliffe." He was a member of the provincial assembly, Justice of the Peace, and Chief Justice of Kent County. However, it is his heir, Lambert Wickes, who is memorialized at a site on Eastern Neck Island believed to be the location of the manor.

The island is now a National Wildlife Refuge where egrets and herons wade around all year and where you might actually spot an osprey's nest. Bogle's Wharf, on the east side, used to be the spot where packet boats called. Today, it is a public landing on the Chester River. You can hunt whitetail deer by lottery (good luck) or wade the flats on the northwest side where you will stumble all over the soft-shell crabs if it's the season. There are trails, a boardwalk and an observation deck for the "birder." So far, two hundred and eighty-five species have been recorded.

Remington Farms, at the entrance to the refuge, offers the good life to wildlife. Don't get confused, there are two refuges on the island, the farm and the refuge. Remington Farms, an experimental breeding ground, has three thousand acres where wildlife coexists with farming. Farmers cultivate a part of the land and supply a portion of the grain they grow to feed the birds and animals in the refuge.

During the War of 1812 only one battle was fought in Kent. Caulk's Field, outside of Chestertown, was the meadow where the British company led by Colonel Peter Parker mounted a diversionary attack on the volunteers. One of Chestertown's finest, Colonel Philip Reed, headed the militia. When the British commander was hit in the leg, his troops turned tail and ran, leaving their commander to die in a farmhouse nearby. He never knew that just before he was hit, the American volunteers had completely run out of ammunition. (Ironic, isn't it?)

There are heroes, and then there are heroines, and Kent has one of the most famous of those females, Kitty Knight. Oh, Kitty was a feisty gal with a hot temper and a will of iron. These characteristics lost her the man she loved and left her somewhat embittered. She was an early starter and set up housekeeping along with two servants, slaves probably, in the red brick house still standing along the Sassafras River in Georgetown--when she was but twelve years of age.

Kitty was ready when the infamous Colonel Cockburn, bane of the Shore during the Revolutionary War, pounded on her front door. The city was ablaze, the houses riffled, the citizens running hither and yon. She faced down the cocky general who was about to set torch to her home shouting, "Burn this house and you burn me with it!" The commander put back, so to speak, by her ferocity. After careful consideration, he retaliated by driving the blade of his boarding axe into her front door. "Come on boys," he shouted and the troops withdrew. He returned, however, and with his men moved in with the headstrong heroine, the belle of Maryland, for the duration. (Must have been pleasant.)

The Kitty Knight story has been embellished as much as the Barbara Fritchie "old gray hair legend" and why not? They are both good yarns. Kitty left this life, but did not desert the house. She likes to rock in the chair in one of the upstairs bedrooms and disturb folks. She has been known to put a curse on visitors, just to be ornery.

Following are a couple of tales told to Robert Allan Gorsuch, Ed. D., and published in Ghosts in Kent County Maryland, a collection of folklore presented to the Graduate Department of Salisbury State College in partial fulfillment of the requirements for the degree of Master of Education.

"One night I was talking to a young fellow in here (the bar at the Kitty Knight House, Georgetown, Maryland) and he just came down from Canada with a brand new sailboat on a trailer. And we were talking in here and two women I knew all got together, sat here at a table and he didn't even go up to his room to check in yet. And he - we were kidding him to begin with and we said, well if there's a rocking chair in the room, put it outside the door because Kitty will be sitting in the rocking chair and rock all night. So he was a little leery and said well how about coming up for a drink and he said, you know, if there's a rocking chair I'll put it outside. I was never up in the rooms before. And sure enough there was a rocking chair in the room. And, so he said he wouldn't put it out in the hall but he would put it in the bathtub. So he put it in the bathtub. As soon as he put it in the bathtub it started to rock. And I think, possibly, a truck or something was coming by at the time and the vibration made it rock, but it did rock. And we just about died laughing because this man was about ready to pack up and leave. So he finally decided he'd take the rocking chair and put it out in the hall for the night. We left him in the room and came on back down here. We were joking about it and all that, and the next morning he got up and got his tractor and trailer, backed it into the unloading part, it was a huge sailboat and a very expensive one, and they put it in the water and it immediately sank. So we said it was the Curse of Kitty Knight.

"So about four weeks later was the next time he was down here and I just happened to be in here at the same time and met him. And he stayed here but nothing happened that night. But when they got the boat to be

158

put over, they had the mast up and the mast fell off and it went right through the bottom of the boat.

"The third time - brand new boats and always from Canada, the third time he came on down it was a storm and he had to go around this way and that way for detours and all that, and of course he didn't realize, in the darkness there's an overhead bridge. It took the whole top off the boat. He was coming down here to stay at the Kitty Knight House. So we kidded him about that. You know, it was the Curse of Kitty Knight. And we haven't seen him since and it's been a year and a half. He was coming down here once a month delivering boats. He said never again." (As told by Florence Price Hague.)

And another, "I made reservations five years ago for a friend of mine from New York. And I didn't have a big enough place for him to stay so I made reservations for him to stay here (Kitty Knight House). And - it was Room 10 - and I dropped him off. It was a Sunday night and he had not been drinking. He wasn't drunk or anything like that. He went upstairs and checked in. He went to bed. It was comfortable, he said, and he went to bed and all of a sudden, he thought he heard the door open and sure enough he opened his eyes and the light from the hall shone in. He saw the door open and close and nobody came in. And the door was locked, so he said. And he got up and made sure the door was locked. He put a chair against the door and a little while later the same thing happened. The door opened and it pushed the chair away from the door. He got up, put the light on and sure enough the chair was over there and the door was closed. He called me on the telephone and said come and get him. He was standing right across the street here with his bags packed. I had to take him all the way up to Route 40 to get a room for the night." (As told by Charles Knapp.)

These days gone by were a time when dueling among men was a common way to validate one's honor. The only place you hear much about duels is on the Eastern Shore. No one would probably have ever heard of General Cadwalader if it weren't for his duel with Thomas Conway, the infamous rogue who led a cabal against the father of our country, George Washington.

This story is told in exactly the same words in every history book dealing with the Shore. General Cadwalader's bullet hit Conway's teeth, knocking them out, but not inflicting a mortal wound. When Cadwalader saw Conway lying on the ground, blood gushing from his mouth (blood **gushing** from his mouth is used in every description). Cadwalader is supposed to have said, "I have stopped the damn rascal's lying tongue at any rate." On his deathbed Conway, as many sinners have been known to do, asked George Washington to forgive him for his conduct. However, the supposed fatal wound proved not to be fatal and Conway recovered and left the country never to be heard from again.

General Cadwalader should have been remembered for his military career, which he undertook with no ambitions as to promotion even resisting all efforts to induce him to take a command, in the Continental Army, but is remembered in Kent County for his contribution to the founding of Washington College.

Civil War feelings ran high against the north in Kent and were barely concealed. (Not at all concealed, actually.) Most of the boys went south to join the Confederate Army. The Union, suspecting that the drowsy little village on the Chester River, Chestertown, might be a breeding place for insurrection, garrisoned the town and successfully kept the lid on.

However, in spite of the County's southern sympathy, it can boast an illustrious list of notables, who served their country, having contributed four United States Senators, also a couple of despicable reprobates, John Frazier--Provost Marshall of Kent County, and Captain Thomas Bradnox--Sheriff and County Justice.

Frazier, a Napoleon-act-alike, took over the town to control the election for which he expected to become, by default if there was no other way, Clerk of the Court in the 1860 election. He declared marshal law, called up the militia and arrested all candidates on the rival ticket, also those who presumed to oppose him. All the prominent men were "captured" and anyone else who got in his way, and imprisoned in the hold of a ship in the river.

He went on to stifle the voice of the press by taking over the newspaper office and forcing the editor to print special notices which told folks that they had to vote for Frazier--or else. (This is all extremely difficult to believe.)

All kinds of protests (is that all?) were launched and there was lots of talk, talk, but little action. Frazier slipped up and neglected to gag the "prisoners" aboard ship. They spilled the beans (sorry trite, but right) by yelling to the Home Guard, who were on a troop ship taking them to Chestertown to vote. Frazier had power and even though charged, he got off with a rap on the knuckles.

Now Captain Bradnox, a villainous type who was described in The Eastern Shore of Maryland and Virginia by Robert L. Swain, Jr., as "ignorant, boorish, a browbeater, a bully and who was unable to sign more than a crude X." The description goes on, "continually in trouble for heavy drinking, embezzling public funds, excessive swearing, disrupting the peace, assault and for causing the death of two servants."

He was accused of beating women, a maid servant in particular, of whom he is supposed to have said, "She did spoil me a batch of bread." He locked up his prisoners for days without food or water. He beat a manservant to death and killed another with repeated blows. (Enough!)

He was also a fool. (You know what lawyers say about people who represent themselves in court? That they have a fool for a lawyer.) He didn't go that far, his wife was the defending attorney. (Probably couldn't get anyone else.) All of this turned out to be irrelevant because he dropped dead before the jury returned the verdict. He would have gotten off anyway because he had passed the "test!" This method of determining guilt was an ancient procedure. If a man touched the corpse of the person he was accused of killing and the body bled, the accused was the real murderer. When Captain Bradnox thrust his fat thumb into the gut of the rigid corpse the flesh only dented, but did not bleed. The result of this somewhat inaccurate method of "testing" for guilt would be

reported to the jury and they would have been compelled to find for the defendant.

Frazier's home, "Frazier Flats," is a spacious brick dwelling, built before the Revolution, along the Choptank River above Dover Bridge. It is considered one of the finest standing structures of Colonial architecture in the area. His home is now in Caroline County, a county that did not exist during Frazier's lifetime.

This confusion, caused by the changing of boundary lines and creating new counties during the first couple hundred years of the Shore's history, can lead to mistakes and uncertainty. Colonel Frazier, who was an official in Kent County, would now be a resident of Caroline County. At least someone is paying taxes on this property to Caroline rather than Kent County.

Even though Kent County is on the Eastern Shore, and not in merry ol' England, there is a subtle code of ethics about the residents, a polite, but reserved attitude, which one supposes harks back to their English heritage. In Chestertown you almost expect to see Sir Lancelot looking for Lady Guinevere or the sire of Kent lurking in the customs house. Kent is definitely a carriage trade town with a lot of class, very upper crust. (Author is attempting to sound very British.)

As you cross the noble Chester River you notice the small cupola-like bridge house, and you know Chestertown is somehow a bit different. The sight of the back porches of these eighteenth century homes, framed by weeping willows whose leaves droop to touch the river, makes you feel comfortable and relaxed. The homes are larger than you would expect. How nice it must have been during the time of the steamboats to sip a mint julep and watch the marvelous paddle wheelers unload passengers. The steamer, B. S. Ford, who always stopped at Chestertown, ran for forty years from Baltimore calling at docks along the Chester and Corsica Rivers. Every one of those landings has rotted away or been torn down.

During the B. S. Ford's forty years on the water she made a lot of friends. From the passengers to the

crew, to the folks in Chestertown, she was special. Today, there is no crew or mate or anyone else around who could give any writer a firsthand account of those days. Therefore, this writer will give you the firsthand account which Hulbert Footner, author of Rivers of the Eastern Shore, got from an old steamboater that he ran into on the beach at Quaker Neck Landing more than forty-five years ago.

"Once on the B. S. Ford, when we was leavin' Bal'more Sunday afternoon at the same time as the Eastern Shore (another line), she almost cut us in two. We was a-backin' out of Pier 7 with three licensed men in the pilothouse, and the Eastern Shore she only had a boy alone in the pilothouse. She struck us just aft our pilothouse. Cap'n of the Eastern Shore got his license suspended for one month, and they passed a law to keep three licensed men in the pilothouse.

"When I was mate on the Corsica, making three trips weekly to Crumpton (Queen Anne's County side of the Chester River) we broke down in the middle of the Bay off Seven Foot Knoll and anchored and blew four whistles for assistance. Tred Avon (now the Oxford Bellevue) was in sight, but her mate didn't hear us and she passed on. By and by a tug with a mud scow come along, anchored the scow and asks us one hundred seventy-five. Cap'n told him to go you know where. Under the law, the tug was forbidden to leave us. So there we stayed looking at each other until he come down in his price to seventy-five and towed us in.

"Remembers a time aboard the B. S. Ford, leaving Baltimore in a heavy nor-easter, lady said to captain, 'Cap'n don't you think it's too risky?' and the Captain said: 'Lady, I think as much of my life as you do.'

"One Christmas Eve when I was mate aboard the Corsica, we lay here at Quaker Neck loading all night with cases of canned goods, oil drums and so forth. At daybreak we started downriver and made Love Point (Queen Anne's) on the ebb tide, and there we run into a heavy nor-easter, which was soon jumping the Corsica's propeller clean out of the water. At Buoy Rock, though we had two passengers, and I and George at the wheel, she wouldn't answer her port wheel and I say to George,

'Hadn't we better head up to Seven Foot Knoll?' but he wouldn't.

"At five-fathoms-lump buoy I seen a puff comin'. Struck us on the starboard bow and knocked her sideto, and she rolled until the water come up to the pilothouse door. She rolled the flagpole right out of her. Down below the passengers was lying on the cabin floor. 'How much more of this have we got to stand?' They was saying. George agreed to turn back to Love Point then. We went back before the wind, ten miles in half an hour! After shifting two hundred cases canned goods astern to keep her screw down, we started out again and made Bal'more by 8 p.m. Which proves two heads is better than one, even if one is a cabbage head. I missed my Christmas dinner.

"Ain't nothin' stopped the Chester River steamboats 'ceppin ice. I mind one winter, when I was on the B. S. Ford as a young fellow, they was four Negroes in the Chestertown jail accused of murder, and the mob was determined to lynch them. So Governor Frank Brown, he ordered them brought to Bal'more, but the B. S. Ford was froze hard and fast to Chestertown Wharf. Now the governor felt bad, because these was young boys and they hadn't any close connection with the murder, so he ordered out the icebreaker Latrobe and he come over across the Bay on her and fetched the boys away without the mob knowing anything. They got to Chestertown 'bout 2 a.m. and went right back, and gemmenie by 9 a.m. in the morning the whole river was froze from shore to shore and men was skatin' across.

"Another time the B. S. Ford was froze to the wharf in Chestertown and some tough fellows came aboard and engaged in a game of poker with the crew down below. There was a fight over the winnings, and during it the Ford caught fire and burned. She was rebuilt, but afterwards she was never allowed to lie at Chestertown.

"The old B. S. Ford come back home a few years ago. They had moved the pilothouse back on top the ladies cabin and taken off the house on the bow. Jes' a barge bein' towed by a goddam tug! Dog my breeches, if it ain't make me feel bad to see that!"

The houses on Water Street were watching events along the river long before the steamboat tooted into view. (If houses could speak, what tales they could tell.) These elegant homes were built and used by wealthy merchants for entertaining and to give their families, who generally lived on farms, a touch of city life. In those days activity centered around the river. Chestertown traded with the English and the West Indies from 1730 to 1775. The surprisingly large customs house was a busy place then. The Flemish bonding makes this building, which dates from the 1760s, extremely sturdy and the glazed headers give the red brick walls a pretty silvery glint.

There is a mystery surrounding a hidden room discovered under the front portion of the customs house. This secret room is made of stone and has a vaulted ceiling with a skylight and wicked looking meat hooks hanging down from the ceiling. The inside door is wrought iron and if the heavy outside door is left open, air can circulate. No one has the foggiest idea what the hidden room could have been used for, perhaps a dungeon? The Kent County historian made a reasonable guess, saying that perhaps it was a place to store contraband. (An educated guess and a good one.)

The Federal style home of Captain John Nicholson is on Queen Street. The write-up, in the walking tour guide, mentions that all three brothers were in the navy. (This offers a bit more information on John, but not much.) If the captain's house could reveal the past, you would be surprised to learn that Chestertown was not always the genteel place it is today. You might even think of it as bawdy.

Hogs, sheep and chickens roamed around New Town, the original name changed to Chestertown in 1780 when the charter was revised. No one paid any attention to the drunken sailors or the animals carousing around Water and up High Street. Lots of cash was lost by young men betting on the horse races at a nearby track or on big-stake poker games. These gay blades took dancing lessons. (We are speaking here, only, of men.) The more aggressive held the sword and yelled "on guard" during fencing classes. They practiced an art form of cursing which put the drunken sailors to shame.

All "good things" come to an end, and as in many other cities on the Shore, laws were passed. In 1732 a law was written to get the big hogs, who were threatening the children, off the streets and into pens where they belonged in the first place. (Seems reasonable.)

It must be understood that hardship and deprivation were to blame for all that occurred in the early days, not only for those on the Shore, but all over Maryland. Even the wealthy had come up the hard way (to use an old phrase). Travel was difficult and communication, as we know it, was nonexistent. There was little contact with the outside world. The thrill of gambling, hunting, horse racing, fencing, dueling, brawling, using offensive language and drinking to excess were outlets that many took. It was well into the next century before this behavior changed a great deal.

When it did, things went from the bizarre to the proper. Old London customs took over and decorum was the order of the day. A high social life echoed the fine British drawing rooms. To be a part of this society required certain things. This new "fancy" took money and the landed gentry had that. The criterion for wealth was applied on the basis of the number of slaves, livestock and the acres of land one owned. If you didn't have lots of wealth you could still be "accepted" if your ancestors had been in the New World long enough or if you had influence--political was best.

Plays, mostly by amateurs, were presented. Music became a passion and grand opera was the vogue, at least for the ladies. Opulent balls and exclusive social functions were fashionable. The militia provided a chance for a man to wave his saber, race his horse and brawl for the fun of it. Off-color stories could be exchanged among the good natured "guys" in the militia without offending.

Now that you know these things, you will want to walk on the somewhat bumpy brick sidewalks of this venerable city and look at the houses where all this took place. Chestertown has the distinction of having one entire block of historic homes, not even Annapolis can claim that.

"Widehall," on Water Street, is absolutely magnificent. This huge, perfectly symmetrical Georgian mansion with five windows on the second floor and three huge dormers on the roof was built in 1769 by Thomas Smythe, a man who was as wealthy as he was illustrious. He had a "summer place" of four hundred acres on Eastern Neck Island, called "Trumpington," which he inherited from his grandfather. (Ah! To have a grandfather who has a summer place.)

Walking around Chestertown can wear down your shoe leather, but there is a feeling, the spell of the history, remembering those who walked these same streets, makes you want to stay and stray around town.

The well-known White Swan Tavern is on High Street where it always was, but not the same one. The first tavern was built in 1733 and in 1793 it was purchased by John Bordley, who enlarged the building and added the touches which gives it the charm it has today.

Another tavern in the town was Worrell's, and this is where George Washington stopped for supper and a night's rest. There is that marker you see lots of places which tells you George Washington dined and lodged there on his return from Philadelphia, on March 20, 1707, while he was president of the United States.

The Wickes Mansion, on High Street, was once a tavern owned by Samuel Beck, the walking guide to Chestertown tells you; but the present owner says it is not so! (So?) Behind the iron fence, enclosing the mansion, is a spectacular garden of boxwood and a grand magnolia tree--a bit of the look of the Ol' South.

Chestertown itself has the feeling of Dixie, a sleepy southern city with folks lolling back in white wicker rockers on the front porches under hanging baskets of pink and white impatiens or out back in the garden houses.

A writer for the Chestertown newspaper, Blain Harden, described Chestertown as "...somewhere between

'Our Town' and 'Main Street', between idyllic neighborliness and claustrophobic provincialism. Norman Rockwell would find plenty to paint and Sinclair Lewis would be busy taking notes." (This author cannot top this description.)

Besides the taverns in town, there are some really amazing renovations. The Geddes-Piper House, now the home of the Kent County Historical Society is a marvel. Not too long ago this building was divided into ten apartments all of which were shabby, to say the least. Now it sparkles with fine wood and furnishings and a cunning collection of tea pots, the treasure of the first owner, the customs collector, William Geddes.

Geddes' brigantine was commandeered when Chestertown had their "tea party." So as not to be forever thought of as a hotbed of Tories, the folks in town decided to have a tea party just like the one in Boston Harbor. On May 23, 1774, they sailed out in small boats, climbed aboard the brigantine and dumped the tea in the Chester River.

Chestertown still has a "tea party" every year. It's fun to be there and watch everyone in colonial garb throwing tea in the water and see the crafts and eat the food and follow along behind the parade and race in the Tea Party Classic Run.

The time to go inside the historic homes is September when the Candlelight Walking Tour takes place. That is when you can gasp at the flicker of candlelight on fine crystal, exquisite silver and English bone china. Here, the oriental carpets show off their intricate patterns against a background of mellowed, hand-pegged floors and lords and ladies greeted the visitors.

"Rock of Ages, cleft for me...," the "Rock of Ages," the Palmer House, is far up High Street in a less than desirable neighborhood. The massive angular stones brought as ballast on Captain Palmer's ship were used to build his home. An engraving of this house was one of Kent County's contributions to the battleship Maryland, when she was launched. Sad to say, the rocks

of ages are covered with whitewash which makes the house difficult to recognize.

Parks are part of Chestertown. The Memorial Park has benches where you might like to sit, as much as the author did, after walking those bumpy bricks, and rest awhile. Eating a Dixie cup of half vanilla and half chocolate ice cream with a wooden scoop and sitting on the bench can take you back to childhood for a time.

Parks used to be a place to meet your friends after school. You rested your books on a bench and chased each other around the monuments or played hide-and-seek among the bushes. The scene from the park is of High Street and the pharmacy where you get the Dixie cup and the bookstore, gift and apparel shops and further up High Street is the Dollar General Store, a part of almost every Eastern Shore city. While you are digging into the ice cream, flavored slightly by the wooden scoop, you might read the engraving on the Civil War Monument.

There was no doubt that Chestertown and Kent County had divided loyalties during the confrontation. The monument reflects this in that one side, the Union portion, reads, "To the soldiers of Kent in the Federal Army 1861-1865," and the names of the dead. The southern side is a bit more earnest. "In commemoration of the patriots and valor of a once divided now restored country to the soldiers of Kent in the Confederate Army 1861-1865" and goes on "under the sun the blue and the gray waiting alike for judgment day."

It is interesting to note the "foreign" battlefields these boys died on: Bunker Hill, Winchester, Manassas, Appomattox, Franklin and Shiloh, places so different than the soft gentle land where they were born. On the list, the first two are brothers, there are other brothers, and even four from one family. You are startled out of your reverie and also delighted at the rapturous sound of a hymn rung every hour by bells in the tower of the Methodist Church.

The sobering experience, at Memorial Park, is forgotten as you watch the lovely lady, Hebe, goddess of youth and beauty and bearer to the Gods, pour

173

sparkling water from a pitcher into the upturned beaks of swans floating in a large bowl. There used to be four big urns around the bowl, but the kids, who like to swim in the fountain, knocked them off so often that the urns were put away for safekeeping. This is Fountain Park, of course, where brick paths, laid out like the spokes of a wheel, lead to the fountain. On summer Saturday mornings the park becomes a market when all of the farmers set up to sell their veggies and fresh flowers. Everyone goes to market and everyone gets a bargain.

On White Horse Farm, outside of Chestertown, is one of the oldest homes in Kent County, a portion built in 1721. A sixteen year old girl, who lived there about two hundred years ago, left her mark. It seems she had a beau not acceptable to her parents. One cold winter night they planned to elope. She rode off into the black of night to meet her intended. Along the lane her horse balked and threw her against a big rock, cracking her skull. The boulder was stained with her blood and has remained so over the years in spite of attempts by future owners to scrub it clean or cover the stain with whitewash.

Besides the bloody rock yarn, there is the ghost tale of Mary Stuart who died January 8, 1803, in her thirty-ninth year. It is said that on the stroke of midnight she seeps up from her grave on the property and walks around the gardens. It used to be that the owner would have ghost parties where all the guests would stand around the grave and one would read the inscription and wait for a "sighting." The waiting got tiresome and the parties were abandoned. (Legend and lore die hard on the Shore. The blood-stained rock is there, however!)

Kent has three hundred years of architecture and it can best be seen and explained in detail on Kent County's Annual Bus Tour. When you "drive" around Kent County with the author, you are going to "see" a lot of what is no longer there.

Rock Hall is like that, even the rockfish are gone. Of all that was there--a couple dozen oyster shucking houses, only one clam and oyster packing plant

is left. Stand on Windmill Point in Rock Hall's harbor and to your left you see the Chesapeake Bay Bridge ten miles away and to your right the sun setting a shocking cadmium red. The harbor reinforces the name; there are a lot of rocks holding back the Bay. The boulders are white, as though perpetually covered with icy crystals. If you are close, you will see that the icy appearance comes from oyster and clam shells...no doubt dumped there by the packing companies.

The area is strung out this way and that. You can get mighty turned around trying to find where it was that you started. Roads end at the water or make circles that lead into another circle and then run out of pavement. City maps are no help since the name of the street is either missing from the maps or from the street. Locals are very helpful, at least they try to be. However, a "piece down the road and left at the place where the Cozy Inn **was**," or some such information, etc., etc., can leave you crazy with frustration. The thought of leaving a row of clam shells behind as a trail to follow in order to get back to where you started, passes through the mind...

The houses scattered under shade trees, not all loblolly pines surprisingly, reminds one of those cottages built on lakes in the 1930s, small and square, with screens on the upper half and wood on the lower portion of the front porches and petunias along the walk. Main Street, if you can find it, is nearly deserted. The "action" is all down by the water.

When travel by water was the way you went, you caught a packet from Annapolis who connected to many landings along the Bay Shore. (You remember Tench Tilghman whose grave is in Oxford?) Tench Tilghman, carrying the news of Cornwallis' surrender at Yorktown, came north on the ferry at Annapolis, crossed to Rock Hall and raced through Kent County toward Philadelphia. Erected by the citizens of Rock Hall is a historical marker, the kind you see along all the highways in America. It was put up in 1932 and tells you that Rock Hall was formerly known as Rock Hall Crossroads, that Main Street is part of the first road in Kent County, in 1675, and that George Washington (another of **those** George Washington signs) passed through here eight known

177

times. The marker is a big one and goes on to say that Tench Tilghman used this road from Yorktown to Philadelphia in October 1781.

The packet made some sense, and there is talk of a hydrofoil making runs from Baltimore to Rock Hall. A good, fast one could do it in twenty minutes. This, of course, would turn Rock Hall back into the boom town it used to be when, not only our first president, but two other presidents, Thomas Jefferson and James Madison went back and forth. They wanted to go to Annapolis, but everyone else now wants to go to Baltimore and spend the day at Harbor Place. (Update--a ferry has just started runs from Baltimore to Rock Hall, but not in twenty minutes, an hour and a half is more like it. Ferries are not hydrofoils.)

Rock Hall will be on the map as long as men put gun to shoulder and shoot wild game. The hunting season, particularly goose season, is big around Rock Hall. The state wildfowl stamps and the additional stamps for hunting deer and turkey bring lots of coins into the State's coffer. This, however, is small change compared to the big bucks spent in Kent County and the town of Rock Hall for accommodations, food, guides and equipment. A new state law became effective July 1988 lowering the bag limit to one duck a day with a limit of two altogether. This ruling has caused a furor among hunters as well as businessmen. The minute the law passed, the phones started ringing and plans to hunt in Kent County were canceled. Under way is a great effort to rescind this law.

Rock Hall is between a rock and a hard place. The fishing industry is all but dead. Developers are banging on the door. The townsfolk want them to disappear, get lost, leave them alone. They want things to stay the same, but things have already changed. If you see the Tolchester Yacht Company, you will know. Forecast for Rock Hall is a Bay front of smart looking condo's and a yacht basin full of astronomically priced sailboats. (Excuse me, yachts.) It won't be all that bad when the cash starts rolling in. Then you can go to the Rock Hall Museum and see how it used to be.

A walk through the museum inside of City Hall, miles down Main Street from where you expect it to be, will tell you the story of the past. This is the finest photographic collection of Tolchester's Amusement Park and the ferries that you will see. Tacked along the wall are pictures of probably every steamboat on the Bay. You recognize the names connected with certain areas. There is a long, about six feet, picture that shows Pratt and Light Streets and Long Wharf in Baltimore in 1912, filled to overflowing with endless rows of steamboats and then, Harbor Place today. (You know it's the same harbor, but it is hard to believe.)

There are several tarnished brass rings from the merry-go-round at Tolchester, and post cards of people looking kind of dowdy, to us, in their attire as they stroll along the midway. They all have smiling faces. A rack of red, yellow and blue birds from the shooting gallery at the amusement park hangs on the wall surrounded by bits and pieces of those days, all hard to distinguish in the clutter. You can see the fire engine red sleigh with a moth-eaten lap robe across the apple green wicker seat because it is so big. There is a box of doorknobs and some ships' lanterns inside a glassed-in area in the middle, a yellowed newspaper with a picture of the primary level graduation class of 1905 is displayed, along with a lace glove and other memorabilia. A piece of rope from what must have been an ocean liner hangs nearby.

A lovely quilt, two actually, are on the wall; there are boat models and a big table with a plasticized mock-up of Rock Hall decorated with the same funny feeling plastic green grass stuff you use to decorate model train setups. Most of what is there has been donated, probably all, and there are tags with the gift giver's name on them. It is crowded and stuffy, even on a cool day, and nothing is very well displayed, but the whole schmear that is the Eastern Shore of Maryland is there.

HARBORS, HARBORS, HARBORS,
BUT WHERE IS ONE,
WHERE ALL CAN COME,
ON A "FOWL" WEATHER DAY,
TO HIDE AWAY.

ROCK HALL HARBOR, I SAY
IS THE PLACE TO STAY.

(The author is not a poet and should know enough not to show it, but she doesn't.)

Somewhere near Rock Hall is the first county seat, New Yarmouth, on Eastern Neck Island. James Ringgold, the guiding light in the founding, settled on a land grant of twelve hundred acres in 1650. He set aside one hundred acres for a government. New Yarmouth was an active trading post with a courthouse, a jail and a couple of taverns and St. Paul's Episcopal Church was nearby. Things went well until tobacco failed as a crop and the warehouses were left vacant. The town continued for a time and then simply vanished, leaving only a name on some yellowed papers. Today, the exact location is unknown. (Ghost towns again!)

St. Paul's Episcopal Church was founded in 1682 and occupied a site on Eastern Neck Island. At the first meeting of the Vestry, records show, it was decided then to construct a new building at Broad Neck Creek, the site of the present St. Paul's Church. The records indicate that a Zachariah Brown agreed to pull down all the timber and clear the churchyard for the sum of twelve hundred pounds of tobacco.

The church on Eastern Neck was abandoned when the Act of 1692 divided the Province of Maryland into thirty parishes and required that the church be centrally located. St. Paul's is the oldest Episcopal Church in continuous use in Maryland. The grounds are spacious and on the ten acres there are glorious oaks, hemlocks, spruces, red-berried holly trees, sycamores and boxwood hedges with that odor you can't forget. The creek is still and peaceful like the graveyard which it borders. The oldest stone marker has this inscription on the headstone.

"Behold & see now here I lye,
As you are now so once was I.
As I am now so must you be,
Therefore prepare to follow me."

(This inscription must have been popular because you see it on other gravestones.)

The most spoken of and searched out grave is that of Tallulah Bankhead who is buried next to her sister under a tree facing the creek. Although not from Kent County, she was a frequent visitor to her sister's farm and so loved it that she requested burial in this peaceful place.

As lovely as St. Paul's is, it is not alone in that, nor does it have the number of intriguing epitaphs that Shrewsbury Episcopal Church does. The church's register dates back to 1695. The present structure is the third built on the site and was constructed using bricks from the original building erected in 1722. Shaded by ancient oaks and with the stone marker of General John Cadwalader just inside the entrance, the church begs a look.

You may read Cadwalader's eulogy, a flowery bunch of nonsense written by his political enemy, Thomas Paine, in a moment of weakness or, perhaps, vindictiveness. One of the most heart-rending epitaphs is: Elizabeth R., daughter of Charles & Sarah, Died Aug. 12, 1876, aged 4 mos. and 18 days. And the poem:

"Little Lizzie was our darling,
Pride of all our hearts and home,
But an angel came and whispered,
Little Lizzie do come home.
Lonely the house and sad the hour,
Since our dear Lizzie has gone,
But, oh a brighter home than ours,
In Heaven is now her own."

The melodic sound of church bells from the chapel's tower can be heard across the countryside. This church bell ringing in Chestertown, and around the County, takes some by surprise--such a nice surprise. Along all the highways in Kent are many modest edifices to God. Mostly, they are painted either red or white and have square, box-like bell towers where the bells are rung by turning a wheel.

Pilot Bay

TOLCHESTER

The previously mentioned Colonel Philip Reed, a soldier of the Revolution and the War of 1812 and the hero of Caulk's Field, is buried at Christ Church I.U. This church dates from 1765 and is near Worton. Not many know what the I.U., worked into the bricks at the back of the building, stands for. A guess is that it comes from a boundary stone nearby that has those letters carved in it.

When you venture into the countryside, particularly in the northwest section, and pass through the tiny settlements here and there you will be struck by how small, small can be.

Route 20 will take you to Tolchester and that is all. This road comes to an end, as you will see! Tolchester Amusement Park was a mystical, magical place, the dream of Captain William C. Eliason. There it was, a glorious, fun-for-all wonderland on the Bay. The long pier was where the steamer Pilot Bay, who could carry six hundred passengers and was always crowded with a parade of summer people, dropped anchor. Sunday school picnickers, ladies in white lawn blouses and floor-length black skirts, their hair piled high atop their heads, hung onto the arm of their man. Little kids, big kids, young folks, old folks, everyone came to Tolchester. The ladies' escorts all wore dark suits, ties and hats with grosgrain bands. It was all very formal as this was an Edwardian resort. Everyone carried wicker baskets slung over one arm filled with biscuits baked with the chicken, deviled eggs topped with stuffed olives, a special treat and a deep-dish sour apple pie.

It was a race to get to the grove and secure a table, one that was near the restrooms and the drinking fountain. Then, hoping the ants didn't crawl into the basket, everyone headed to the arcade. Two, three-story towers with red roofs were at each end of the arcade at the foot of the pier.

The hawkers kept up a steady chant, "Hit a duck, three shots for a dime, ten for a quarter." If you hit a wooden duck five times in a row, you won a U.S. Cavalry revolver. Few were that good, but some could actually make the bell ring. "Around and around the big

wheel goes, where it stops nobody knows. Step up gents, win a kewpie doll for your sweetie." The wheel had fifteen numbers, making the odds attractive for the carnival con man.

The girls liked to ride a lion or a giraffe while the boys stuck to the prancing horses that followed each other around and around on the merry-go-round. After a while you went back to the shady picnic grove, laid face up on the grass, and rested as you listened to the clang of the orchestra's cymbals playing "Strike up the Band" and other martial music. You never rested long, and soon you were up and back on the rides.

The ferris wheel rose so high that you could see the steamboats, <u>Emma Giles</u>, the <u>Lewis</u> and the <u>Tolchester</u>, way out on the Bay, bringing Baltimorians to the park for a Sunday outing.

If you were twelve years old and very brave, you took your gal on the "DIP," the scariest roller coaster ever. The cars moved so slowly to the crest, and then, like a jet plane, dove straight down heading right for the Chesapeake Bay; all the girls screamed. Up, down and around, you jerked and held onto the bar until your knuckles were white. Near the end of the tunnel, where it was dark, you had a chance to smooch with your honey.

Oh! It was a good time! Some folks stayed at the hotel on the hill above the arcade. Tolchester was a flashy summer resort until the steamboats ceased their daily runs across the Bay, and then the lights went out.

Some, who remember, will tell you about the dirt lane which led you, in your horse-drawn buggy, to Tolchester, if you lived on the Bay side. You were mighty dusty when you got there. The road is black-topped now and has a chain-link fence on each side. As you reach the water, there is a slight rise. If you want to get a little closer to see where the landing was, do, but be careful. When you reach the crest of the rise, and go over, there is nothing to stop you from driving straight into the Bay. It is quite a surprise to see the road heads downhill and disappears under the water. There is no barricade, not even a couple sawhorses. The sign, just before you pass over the

186

rise, reads "DEAD END!" and they are not kidding! The beach is a driftwood collector's heaven but can only be reached by wading around the fence at low tide. The driftwood is the only prize at Tolchester today, no Kewpie dolls, no U.S. Cavalry revolvers. The grandstand has survived to make one last stand at St. Michaels Maritime Museum in Talbot County. The whole place was sold at public auction in 1963.

Heading north on Route 298 you see flat farm land with the barns and silos clustered together in the middle of maybe one hundred acres of fertile fields. Along the way you will come to Fairlee, a fairly tiny cluster of homes. At the crossroads you spot a general store, no--two general stores, one on one side of the road and the other across the highway. One calls itself a five-star general store, the other, just general. Inside the five-star store there is a counter and a cooler with juices, milk, eggs, soft drinks, oleo and butter and around it a few shelves with cereals and crackers and that's about it. Across from five-star is general, with no counter, but the rest is about the same. A large styrofoam cup of coffee is 50 cents and there is 3 cent bubble gum for the kids.

Worton, on down the road, seems to be an area rather than a town. The area where the Kent County High School is located. Apparently, this centrally-located school services all of Kent County. (How many high schools are in the county in which you live?) Worton Park is the first of its kind in the County, you are told. There is an athletic complex with a semiprofessional ball field, and space for lacrosse, soccer and whatnot.

Lynch is the beginning or the ending of the nineteenth century railroad towns in Kent County depending on where you are coming from. The main, and only, street in Lynch runs straight as an arrow across the railroad track. The crossing has no gates, nor do any others around here, so beware. Beside the track is a very large grain company, very large. No people around, though. (It's eerie, you never seem to see the inhabitants of these crossroad towns.)

There is a post office about as large as the stamps sold there. Next door is a store with a Coca-Cola sign hanging on a green metal post in front of the white frame cottage, and an "open" sign in the window...but the store is closed. You are comforted to read the zip code and the name, Lynch, on the front of the post office, at least you know where you are.

A string of railroad towns ran from Massey through Millington to Kennedyville, Lynch, and Worton, with little spurs here and there. Freight trains still use these tracks so, again, keep an eye out lest you get snagged on their cow catcher.

Lynch wasn't always famous for its silos or the railroad. Once there was a lumber yard and construction company. They worked together and were a buzzing business. Worton was a milk station (?) and remained so until recently. Millington was actually written about by Folger McKenzie, the "Bentztown Bard" of Baltimore.

He visited this mill town and wrote, "...gracious welcome as you come into this old town on the far edge of Kent County." (Well, that is something, isn't it?) A four-corners town where Sassafras and Cypress Streets meet has spread out to include a fire department, a school, several churches, a bank and some active businesses that do not have open signs in the window when they are closed.

They say, and you should believe, that the town of Millington was built on a tract of land granted to David Massey in 1754. Thomas Gilpin, however, founded the town and he called it Gilpinton. He was a naturalist, (an early environmentalist), who produced a strain of wheat which wouldn't mildew. This was very important if you were shipping grain to the West Indies, and it made Mr. Gilpin a lot of dough, not flour dough, **cash** dough.

In spite of all his "dough," it didn't buy him the town's name. The place soon became known as Bridgetown, **then** Head-of-Chester, **then** in 1827 because of the many mills, not lumber mills remember but flour mills, the official name became Millington. But not because of the

mills, no--because of Robert Millington. The reason--
because the town extended onto his farm and he built
one of the earliest houses. (It pays to get there
early.)   There is one fascinating house, really
fascinating. This old place has been pushed back so far
into the past that the front steps have been cut off to
allow a wider sidewalk which leaves the front door
hanging.

Getting away from railroad towns and their pasts,
we look for the still pond, after which the town of
Still Pond is named. It began as Steel's Pone (meaning,
in Elizabethan English, favorite).   Steel, an early
settler, took up life around the still pond. Definitely
a still spot along the highway, but pretty, a gentle
place where people can actually be seen.   One was
washing mud from his truck. When asked, "Where is the
pond or creek the town is named after?" "'Bout two mile
down, by the Coast Guard Station," he mutters. You risk
another question! "Is the pond called "still" because
it has no bottom?" "'Bout right," is your answer. The
pond is purported to be a place for spooks, who do well
in bottomless places. (Still ponds run deep and
mysterious things go on.)

The following tales were told to Robert Gorsuch,
Ed. D., by William E. Price, Florence Price Hague and
William Pippin.

"When I was a young man I was coming back home in
a horse and carriage, down by Still Pond Creek, on a
dirt road. A light came up in front of me and paused
in front while the horse reared. The ball of light then
came up over the horse, me and the carriage, and went
down in back of me. I took off for home but never knew
what it was."

"Pop used to tell us the story about him and mom
and some of us kids riding in the carriage going to the
store when a ball of fire came up out of the bushes near
Still Pond Creek and hit the horse in the side. The
horse reared up and took off for home. When we got home
pop looked at the horse and it had all the hair burned
off where the ball of fire had hit."

Another crossroads town is Galena which, naturally, wasn't its original name. It was Downs Crossroads, for the usual reason, roads crossed there, and the land was owned by William Downs. Putting that information aside, no one knows where the name Galena came from except from the streak of silver found on a nearby farm. Galena means, in mineralogy, native lead sulfide from which silver is obtained, nicknamed "horn" silver in these parts. The silver was sent to Philadelphia where it was formed into shoehorns, buckles and spoons. Galena has some fame as a popular place for ghosts.

"Years ago a farm near Galena had large fields planted in asparagus. This vegetable requires much hand labor to harvest it. He hired fourteen Negro men for the job, some of them coming from as far away as Baltimore. These men were housed in small cabins on the farm.

"After the day's work, these men often walked to the nearest colored settlement, which was just outside Galena. The shortest distance to the settlement was across the fields. To get to the settlement, they had to cross an adjoining farm. The farms were separated by a fence running the length of the fields.

"One night as one of the workers was making his way across the fields, he saw a headless rider on a horse, riding along the fence. He was sure the headless rider was the former owner of the adjoining farm out looking over his property. He watched and listened as the sound of the horse's hoofs faded away in the distance.

"When he got back to the cabins, he told the others what he had seen. After this, whenever the others went this way, they saw the headless rider, too.

"One man decided he would do away with the rider which he felt sure was the ghost of the man who had owned the other farm. One night he carried a pistol with him. As the rider approached, the man fired. The rider caught the bullet and threw it back at the man, making it whiz so close that it grazed the man's ear.

"Needless to say, this was the end of their crossing the fields. They followed the road after this, even though it was a much longer distance."

"The story was told me in 1937 by a Mr. James P. Davis who is now deceased. He has a son living in Galena by the name of Julian Davis. But the story as it was related to me is that he had been courting his wife and as was his custom, he came across this same road coming home. And he had obviously sort of drifted off - back in those days the horses, on roads they knew, would find their own way. But something woke him up this night. The horse got to snortin' and a blowin' and jumpin'. It was one of those nights the moon was out but it was cloudy - clouds goin' across the face of the moon - and there is a bad curve and a bridge in the bottom. Of course in those days I imagine it was just a stream you could ford. And he says when they got down there the horse got carrying on so bad that he had the reins in his hand and was pullin' and haulin' on the horse, and there was a horseman on a horse. And as he got even with him - you couldn't hear the horse - he could see that he had no head. He said he was very upset and scared beings he was a man maybe in his twenties. But he said he never saw it again. That's all I can tell you." (If there were two sightings, there must be a headless horseman riding around Kent County somewhere.)

Better see Betterton, it is worth it. As you come into town, a town of respectable size, in contrast--that is to others in Kent, there is a green and red sign which tells you that Betterton is the jewel of the Chesapeake. At the end of this street and over a hill is the Bay.

Around 1900 one of the old houses in Betterton was torn down and underneath the floors were skulls! No one knows whose skull is whose, but the historian tells you that some folks believed this was a way to keep ghosts from your house. This practice has lost out to ghostbusters who exterminate for a small fee, but they don't guarantee their work.

Fishermen used to mend their nets down along the old dock where an early movie house was put up by some enterprising soul. It was about 1930. The films were advertised as "high class." The Port Washington docked at this pier as late as the 1970s.

In the early days the Hotel Rigby sat atop the hill overlooking the water. You can still see a part of the concrete steps to the hotel and just make out the faded black letters, Becker's Beach, painted on the steps. The hotel ran the length of the strip and was considered a many-faceted diamond, class hostelry.

You ask a Bettertonian what she remembers best and she tells you, "the three flags on top of the post office, the excitement in town when the steamboat whistled its arrival and the wonderful carousel with the prancing ponies." But best of all she remembers "the wonderful taste of Miss Kitty Kaufman's marvelous milkshakes."

The name Betterton is in honor of Elizabeth Turner Betterton, who was a force to be reckoned with. She was a mover and a shaker and pushed and pushed until all the homes in town were Bed and Breakfasts. She was married to Richard Turner and there is a Turner's Creek nearby. The name must have come from the Turner family, but no one offers this information.

Down by the water there is a small park with a bit of grass, a bathhouse (a nice one) and shade under a couple big ol' trees. You can lie on your back and look at the cloudless blue sky, just like they used to do in Tolchester. This resort was much the same with the ferris wheel and a merry-go-round and the games of chance and the pink cotton candy and all that made these spots on the Bay special.

One word of warning to all who are unfamiliar with Bay Beaches--if you touch toe to water you may get the horrid disease, urticaria! This scourge of the body does not terminate immediately, it takes forever--it seems, to get the burning sting of the (naughty word) nettles out of your system. They infect all Chesapeake Bay water everywhere, everywhere! Nettle nets help, but it's nicer to sit in the sun and look at the water than it is to go in and run out screaming, nettle nets aside. In the summer, there is often a cart with hot dogs and fresh-squeezed lemonade that quenches thirst like nothing else. A shady spot to rest, if you're just passing through and don't have your yard chairs in the trunk, is the bench along the front of the bathhouse.

There are views all over Chesapeake Country. But where, tell me where, can you see the cliffs of Cecil County rising on your right, the fresh waters of the Sassafras, Elk and Northeast Rivers mixing with the Bay, and on clear bright days, the Susquehanna River at Thomas Point? Where is it that a local man, leaning against the wall near you, tells you that for over fifty years the light house at Thomas Point has been "manned" by a female! (The friendly local, said "manned" by a female, somehow that doesn't sound right. "Manned," but could he have said "womaned?" I suppose not, but the feeling was, A WOMAN--JUST IMAGINE!)

Another pretty spot on the Bay is Turner's Creek Park. The Kent Museum is on the right as you head for the water. A red metal barn-like building is filled with a collection of early farm tools, not rakes and hoes, but the big stuff, combines and tractors and wooden thrashing machines with muddy wheels, as though they had just come in from the fields. There is a one-man saw, a corn chopper and the conveyor belt that carried the corn. There is only one, each, of the big stuff, but one is enough; they take space. A red wagon is brought out and stuffed with sweet hay when Kent Museum has its "day." Folks take rides, get hayseed in their hair and dirt under their fingernails, but you're so close to the Bay you can always run down and wash your hands, watching closely for those infamous globs of jellyfish who don't care one bit if your fingers are dirty.

Old Charlie's house is there by the museum. Charlie was a slave and the house he lived in was, no doubt, as decrepit then as it is now. Plans are to renovate this shack...someday. Two families shared this two-story tiny abode. The "apartments" were divided right down the middle by a steep staircase with risers so narrow you have to step sideways to get to the loft rooms.

Outside, by the barn in the fresh air, sitting on wooden floats, is an old fishing shanty. It is (I must say) adorable with the sooty black stovepipe sticking through the roof and the tiny oval window. This little cottage would have made a nice playhouse for a child, but it never was. This house went to sea. It provided shelter on bitter winter days when fishing for an existence, rather than for pleasure, made it necessary to fish on the bleak frozen days of winter.

Down where you washed your hands is the old grist mill which helped keep the Eastern Shore famous as the breadbasket of the Revolutionary War. Again, there are plans to make this building into a bathhouse sometime... This park is like others, except it is on the Chesapeake Bay and has a view and a pavilion and a sandy beach. Up on the top of the hill, where the view is best, was where Captain John Smith, who was everywhere, came to visit. (He got around almost as much as the father of our country, he just didn't sleep ashore.) However, he did come ashore and right on this very hill he stood face to face with the Chief of the Cantayks Indians! This was in 1608. The date is documented, but what is not documented, is why he was there, and what was said. (Oh well.)

This park is the place where wishes come true. As you stand on the hill overlooking the mother of Bays, drop a coin in the wishing well. If you make the right wish, it will come true. Wish to return again to Kent County and Maryland's Eastern Shore, this place apart, and you will.

USEFUL INFORMATION

Geddes-Piper House, Church Alley, Chestertown. May-October, Saturday-Sunday, 1-4pm. Admission.

Eastern Neck National Wildlife Refuge, Route 445, south of Rock Hall. Daily, sunrise-sunset.

Rock Hall Museum, South Main Street, Municipal Building, Rock Hall. Wednesday-Sunday, 2-4pm.

Kent Museum, Route 448, Turner's Creek Public Landing, near Kennedyville. April-September, 1st and 3rd Saturdays, 10am-4pm. Admission.

Remington Farms, Route 20, north of Rock Hall. Free driving tour brochure available. February-late October, daylight hours.

Washington College, Washington Avenue, Chestertown. Daily, 9am-5pm.

St. Paul's Episcopal Church, off Route 20, past Remington Farms between Chestertown and Rock Hall. Daily, 9am-5pm.

Shrewsbury Parish Church, Route 213, north of Kennedyville. Daily.

For information and guides on Kent County and Chestertown write: Kent County Chamber of Commerce, P.O. Box 146, 118 N. Cross Street, Chestertown, Maryland 21620, or phone (301) 778-0416.

ABOUT THE AUTHOR

If you have read Volume I of **Maryland's Eastern Shore, A Place Apart**, you already know that Jacqueline Heppes Baden is a free-lance writer and illustrator with over 40 pieces on Maryland alone published in the Gaithersburg Gazette newspapers; that she produced two audio tour cassettes on central and southern Maryland, that she has two sons, five grandchildren and lives in Rockville, Maryland.

What you may not know is her reason for writing Volumes I and II. Most Marylanders race pell-mell along Route 50 heading for Ocean City never giving a thought to what they might be missing along the way. That is the reason Jackie wrote the book! After thirty years of heading straight for the city by the sea, she got off and took a look. What she found is enclosed between the covers of Volumes I and II in hopes that after reading the books others will also take a look.

Jackie's horizons have broadened since her days at Hood College as a continuing education student. She is a member of the International Women's Writing Guild, the Writer's Center in Bethesda, Maryland, and the Eastern Shore Writers' Association. Plans are to continue the series of books on all the counties in Maryland.

Volume III, on the western Maryland counties of Washington, Allegany and Garrett, will be released in June 1991 followed soon by the southern Maryland counties of Charles, St. Mary's and Calvert. She hopes by writing the series of books on Maryland's counties that Marylanders will better know their state, often referred to as "America in Miniature."

SOURCES CONSULTED

Adler, Georgia, (Director), _For God and Country: The Hambleton Family of Maryland_.

Augustine, Betty, D. Morris, and Bettie H., _Pemberton Historical Park Guidebook_.

Ayers, Bonnie Joe, _Maryland Magazine_, 20th Anniversary Issue.

Bjerke, Gene, "Messenger of Victory", _Chesapeake Bay Magazine_, October 1989.

Bryon, Gilbert, _St. Michaels: The Town That Fooled the British_.

Burgess, Robert H., _This Was Chesapeake Bay_.

Chapelle, Howard Irving, _The Chesapeake Bay of Yore_.

Clark, Charles B., _The Eastern Shore of Maryland and Virginia_.

Footner, Hulbert, _Rivers of the Eastern Shore_.

Gorsuch, Robert Allan, Ed.D., _Ghosts in Kent County Maryland_.

Historical Society of Talbot County, _For God and Country, The Hambleton Family of Maryland_.

Horton, Tom, _The Bay Country_.

Janson-LaPalme, Robert J., _Chestertown: An Architectural Guide_.

Kent County Bicentennial Committee, _Kent County Guide_.

Kessey, Lori, _Recollections of a Seaside Village_.

Knust, Karl B., Jr., _The Werewolf Pilot of the Eastern Shore and Other Stories About Supernatural Events in Modern Times_.

SOURCES CONSULTED

Loftus, Michael J., (Editor), Commemorating the 200 Anniversary of Caroline County.

Mullikin, James C., Ghost Towns of Talbot County.

Oldham, Sally G., Historic Preservation in American Communities.

Papenfuse, Stiverson, Collins, and Carr, Maryland A New Guide to the Old Line State.

Queen Anne's Historical Preservation Committee, The Colonial Courthouse at Queenstown.

Queen Anne's Historical Society, History of Caroline County.

Queen Anne's Historical Society, I Remember When...

Scharf, John Thomas, History of the Eastern Shore of Maryland.

Smith, Doe, "Rock Hall North of the Chester River", Chesapeake Bay Magazine, August 1988.

Smith, Jane Ockershausen, The Maryland One-Day Trip Book.

Tilip, Fay and Ray, Chesapeake Fact, Fiction & Fun.

Tucker, Jane Foster, Jeremiah Banning Marine and Patriot.

Tucker, Jane Foster, A Port of Entry Oxford, Maryland.

Walbert, Marian, Kent County Maryland.

Other sources are: assorted walking tour guides, brochures and material available through the Department of Tourism and Economic Development for the counties and the state of Maryland.